Praise for *Insia*

"If you want to be challenged, comforted, informed, and transformed by a fresh encounter with Jesus and his miracles, then this is an excellent place to start."
—**Dr. Ben Witherington**, Amos Professor for Doctoral Studies, Asbury Theological Seminary

"An incredible book that will help twenty-first-century Jesus followers make sense of first-century miracles: engaging the mind while maintaining the awe and wonder of God's supernatural work."
—**Rachel Billups**, Executive Pastor of Discipleship, Ginghamsburg Church, Tipp City, Ohio

"Jessica LaGrone combines the careful observation of a scientist with the rhetorical artistry of a poet to craft this study of Jesus' miracles. I learned for the first time how his miracles are often in response to our desperation. Excellent for group study and for individual reflection."
—**Talbot Davis**, Pastor of Good Shepherd UMC in Charlotte and author of *Head Scratchers* and *Crash Test Dummies*.

Jessica LaGrone

Inside
the
Miracles
of
Jesus

Discovering *the*
Power *of* Desperation

Abingdon Press
Nashville

Library of Congress Cataloging-in-Publication Data

Names: LaGrone, Jessica, author.
Title: Inside the miracles of Jesus : discovering the power of desperation / Jessica LaGrone.
Description: Nashville : Abingdon Press, [2018] | Includes bibliographical references.
Identifiers: LCCN 2018015665 (print) | LCCN 2018042553 (ebook) | ISBN
 9781501870798 (ebook) | ISBN 9781501870781 (pbk.)
Subjects: LCSH: Despair—Religious aspects—Christianity. | Jesus Christ—Miracles.
Classification: LCC BT774.5 (ebook) | LCC BT774.5 .L34 2018 (print) | DDC 232.9/55—dc23
LC record available at https://urldefense.proofpoint.com/v2/url?u=https-3A__lccn.loc.gov_2018
015665&d=DwIFAg&c=_GnokDXYZpxapTjbCjzmOH7Lm2x2J46Ijwz6YxXCKeo&r=ox0wiE5wy
qlD4NWBvXI_LEW57Ah1_xv-dTElReAYRyw&m=ejU_5xSt_RC-sz0E5rqwtupky32zVNC9YY
-BKXdsODw&s=e-JNf7i8nQblPZskgzmNAGUNBwRpECTO_IGpUXxw-pQ&e=

19 20 21 22 23 24 25 26 27 28—10 9 8 7 6 5 4 3 2 1
MANUFACTURED IN THE UNITED STATES OF AMERICA

CONTENTS

INTRODUCTION

When was the last time you felt desperate? Sometimes we stand right in the middle of a desperate situation, and sometimes we carry around with us a low-grade desperation. But we all know that feeling of being at the end of ourselves, at the end of our own strength, and reliant on the power, compassion, and love of God to save us.

I remember a day when desperation became my overpowering companion. My friend Laura and I had signed up to go on our first ever overseas trip to Israel. While the rest of the group we were traveling with had booked a connecting flight from our home in central Kentucky to a major international airport north of us, we thought we'd be frugal by simply driving the few hours to that airport and parking at a friend's house nearby. We were excited and packed and felt fully prepared and ready to go—until we checked the weather report. A major winter weather system had moved across our path, leaving the roads ahead icy and treacherous. I'll never forget how tightly I gripped the steering wheel on that long, long drive. Laura and I were both from the South and had never driven on ice-covered roads. The journey was slippery and slow, littered with cars that had skidded off the road. My heart rate stayed so high I think it must have counted as cardio exercise even though

INTRODUCTION

I was sitting down! I don't think I've ever prayed so hard or spent such a long car trip in silence as we did that day, but we made it to our destination. Our friends were ready to greet us, having relaxed on their trouble-free regional flight while we were inching along the road below. Laura and I had a unique perspective as we journeyed to the Holy Land. We entered the rest of that trip, knowing God was with us because we had already been clinging to him just to get started.

Desperation often means that we have come to the end of ourselves. We are out of resources and places to turn. The power of desperation moves us to action and can even give us the boldness to do what needs to be done, to go that last mile, or to sacrifice that last bit of energy to get the thing we need most. Sometimes it means running completely out of inner resources and turning to the help only God can supply.

In the following chapters, we'll witness Jesus demonstrate the presence and power of God by performing miracles in some very desperate moments. He turned water into wine at a wedding party on the verge of ruin, healed sick people who had no more options but his healing power, calmed a storm with his words, opened blind eyes, and even raised the dead. While these beloved stories draw our attention to divine power, they also have something else in common: human desperation. Every time we see Jesus performing a miracle, we also get a glimpse into the gift of desperation, a gift that opens us to the dramatic power of God through our desperate need for him.

Sometimes I wish I had been there with Peter and James and John and the others to see Jesus's miracles in person. I wish I had gotten to witness the moment in Mark 4:39 when Jesus called out, "Peace! Be still!" and the wind and the waves of the storm stopped immediately in response to his words or the time there was so little food to go around, but in Jesus's hands, next to nothing became everything that was needed to feed more than five thousand people. I wish I had been there to see the joy in the eyes of the people who were healed, the surprise of Peter as he stepped out onto the water, or the amazement of Lazarus as he came out of his tomb alive again.

But as much as those particular miracles impress and amaze me, they all point to a greater miracle—the Miracle of miracles, Jesus himself.

As impressive as Jesus's signs and miracles are, Jesus himself is our destination. He is the home we've been longing for, the end of the road we have been following the signs of these miracles toward. It may be our desperation that leads us to him, but it's our love that keeps us with him.

I'm not sure if you've been aware or not, but even *you* are part of a miracle. You are part of the grand miracle story of Jesus's rescue. Within the big story are smaller, particular stories of restoration, healing, wholeness, and wonder. But the overarching story is the miracle of God's rescue plan for his beloved children.

The miracles of Jesus help us see that our weakness is an invitation for God to work powerfully in our lives, reminding us that we need God on our best days just as much as we do on our worst.

Would you give God permission to work in your heart and life? Offer yourself to him and express your desperate desire to know him more intimately and to see his power at work in your life—on your best days as well as your worst days. He is a God who still works miracles!

Jessica LaGrone

CHAPTER 1

The Gift of Desperation

What Happens When We Run Out

Miracles started out for me as a problem to be solved.

I'm a scientist by training. I spent much of my undergraduate years in a science lab: experimenting, observing, and writing up hypotheses about the evidence found. About halfway through college I experienced a radical change of direction that took me from medicine to ministry. God got my attention in some pretty significant ways—some of which I would even call miraculous—communicating that I'd be serving him in ministry, not medicine. But even though my calling changed, the way my brain works did not.

Here's what I mean: I'm still pretty analytical by nature, and sometimes I find myself applying the scientific method to the work of ministry. I've even caught myself approaching pastoral counseling as if experimenting in a lab! (There's nothing more comforting than pouring your heart out to your pastor about your problems and hearing this response, "Well, let's lay out the possible variables in this system and hypothesize the quantitative change they might enact on the observed outcomes.")

OK, so I don't actually say it out loud, but I do sometimes have a hard time remembering that human nature is not a scientific or measurable quantity. I've discovered, though, that God made me just the way I am—analytical and science-minded—and God has plans to use every bit of who I am to serve him. I had an idea of who I was and what I would do with my life; who I am didn't change, but God had in mind something very different for me to do. Even when God changes the direction of our lives, he still uses the way we're wired to serve him.

When I read the miracle stories in the Bible, I sometimes find myself putting my scientist's hat on. Scientists ask questions and look for answers, and I have a lot of questions.

I sometimes wish I could have stood next to Moses as the Red Sea parted, holding a tensiometer to measure the surface tension of the water as it pulled away from gravity, or beside Jesus at Cana with my test tube to find out just how H2O (water) could possibly become CH3CH2OH (ethyl alcohol). I would like to have put monitors on Lazarus to see his vital signs as the "beep beep" of a heartbeat appeared where once there was none.

I'm in good company. We see many people in the Bible asking questions about God's miraculous acts and his promises to do amazing, seemingly impossible things. In Exodus 3 and Luke 1 we see that Moses, Zechariah, and Mary had questions too. When it comes to the miraculous, we tend to ask two common questions.

1. *How?* My own desire to measure miracles is really birthed out of a desire to answer the many questions they raise. Most of my questions about the miracles are *how* questions. How are these things possible? How do miracles occur? How did God do that?

2. *Why?* The deeply emotional side of me (it's in there battling it out with the analytical side) also has questions about miracles. Mostly they begin with the word *why.* "God, why was this person miraculously healed while a child died?" "Why did you bring some people back from the dead

while others such as your earthly father, Joseph, or your cousin John the Baptist died during your lifetime?" "Why do you answer some prayers for miracles and not others?" If you are like me, at one time or another you have found yourself staring out into the sky as you cry out to God, "Why?"

We all have *how* and *why* questions. They are part of our human experience and curiosity, and in truth, they are sometimes what drives us to God for answers. But when I read the Bible, it seems that the *how* and *why* questions aren't the first ones to be answered. Most often, we see miracles answering the question of *who*. I believe it's the *who* question that puts the *how* into perspective and gives us a relationship with the One who walks with us through our *why* moments in life.

What are the *who* questions that we're talking about?

The disciples' question, "Who is this . . . ?" is the beginning point of the *who* question. Who is this man who can still the wind and the waves, turn water into wine, heal a blind man, and raise the dead? But as we read story after story of God's great acts on earth, we begin to ask the psalmist's question, "Who is like the LORD our God?" (Psalm 113:5). The answer is clear: *no one*. No one is like him. No one whom I've ever met before. I've never seen anyone walk on water. I've never encountered anyone who could make a river turn to blood. I've never met anyone who speaks through whirlwinds, burning bushes, and descending doves. I've never seen anyone heal blindness with a touch.

The miracle stories describe a God who is like no one else. They often leave us in awe and wonder. They reveal many things about God, but first and foremost they remind us that God is *transcendent*. God transcends (surpasses, goes beyond, rises above) all that we see and understand. Nothing in our finite, earthly experience prepares us to understand what kind of being God is and what he is capable of. When God speaks in miracles, it tells us that he is beyond everything we understand about our world and our capabilities in it.

A transcendent God, by definition, is hard to see, to touch, to

3

understand, and most significantly, to know. But what if you were a transcendent, all-powerful God who *wanted* people to know you? What if you were a creator trying to have a deep and personal relationship with those in your creation? How would you go about it? Would you boom with a thundering voice so that your power was heard loud and clear? Would you shake the foundations of the ground so that those you had created sensed your presence?

Most demonstrations of power that you might try would probably be so frightening that no one would stick around long enough to find out what you were trying to say! It's no accident that so many encounters with God and his messengers in Scripture begin with, "Do not be afraid." To encounter God's power is a frightening experience!

I remember a story a youth minister told me when I was a teenager that helped me make sense of how God answers the *who* question for us. If you were standing above an anthill, watching the ants scurry to and fro about their work, and you were overcome with a deep love for those ants and wanted to tell them that you loved them, how would you go about telling them? I initially got stuck on this part of the story because, growing up in Texas, I had been stung by my fair share of fire ants and couldn't imagine why anyone would love ants!

You could stand over them and shout, "I love you!" at the top of your lungs, but they wouldn't understand you. You could write a tiny letter and deliver it with tweezers to the center of the colony, but they couldn't read it. But if you happened to have supernatural powers, the one way you could communicate your love for the ant colony would be to become an ant yourself—to take on an ant body, learn to speak ant language, and walk into the colony looking and speaking exactly as they did in order to connect with them and tell them of your love.

The ability to translate yourself into the physical world in such a tangible, relatable, understandable way is called *immanence*, and it is the opposite of transcendence. This is the way of Jesus: to take the incomprehensible, invisible nature of God and package it in a way we can touch, feel, hear, and see.

Desperation isn't a preferred or pleasant condition, but it's the stuff that miracles are made of.

By taking on human flesh, Jesus gave us a God we can comprehend (immanence). But within that flesh, as John 1:14 says, "We have seen his glory" (transcendence). The transcendent power of God acted through this first-century Jewish man.

Transcendence without immanence produces fear: God is terrifying, unrelatable, unknowable. Immanence without transcendence produces casual overfamiliarity and contempt: Jesus becomes my buddy; he is just like me, and nothing in particular about my life has to change because he is part of it. However, Jesus is the perfect balance. Fully God. Fully man. This is the Incarnation: the fullness of God putting on the fullness of human nature, the supernatural and the natural meeting in one incredible person.

If this seems a little mind-boggling for you, you're not alone! The Incarnation causes just as many questions for us as it provides answers.

People read the stories of Jesus, and he appears so normal, so human. How could someone so seemingly natural do these supernatural things? This means that people are more skeptical of Jesus's miracles than many other parts of the Bible. They're often searching for the hidden trick in the miracle, the secret hoax or conspiracy embedded in the stories. This happens to me, too, when the *how* questions get a little out of control and begin to take priority.

Sometimes as I pray and offer God my own needs and the needs of the people I love deeply, I begin to ask how questions. Lord, *how* are you going to meet this financial need? *How* are you going to turn my loved one's life around? *How* are you going to right all the wrongs that I see around me? And if I'm not careful I also begin to answer my own questions, trying to help God out by telling him just how to handle all the problems I've put before him! The *how* questions sometimes end up with me putting myself in God's place and dictating instructions to the King and Creator of all things. *How* often leads me down a road that's less than helpful for me—and I'm sure from God's perspective as well. I sometimes find myself in a whirlwind of *whys* and *hows* and forget the God at the center of the whole story.

Instead, the question to ask first when you meet a miracle is the question of *who*. After all, God didn't come to earth in person to give us the *how* secrets behind his power. And although God knows that the pain of the *why* is often deeply personal and important, his deepest longing is for us to ask the *who* question that will lead us like paving stones straight into the only relationship that can make sense of the *whys* we face.

Who is the question that will take us onto the boat with the disciples, gasping at the moment a raging storm stops cold. It's the question that transports us to a tomb, staring into the tear-streaked face of a grieving friend who speaks the commanding words: "Lazarus, come out!" (John 11:43). It will lead us to look into the eyes of compassion that see the soul of a hurting person, while others see a dirty leper, an outcast woman, a blind beggar.

Asking the question "Who is this?" about the God behind the miracles will lead not only to answers but also to a person. Every single miracle teaches us something about the transcendent God and lead us closer to him. After all, the One who walked on water, healed the lame, made the blind see, and raised people from the dead is alive and present with you as you read these stories, and he longs to be in relationship with you. Every miracle story in this book is an invitation into relationship with the God who bends low to meet us right where we are—in the middle of our most desperate moments. As we'll see over and over again as we explore Jesus's miracle stories, the very real presence of desperation leads to an encounter with the very real power of Jesus, resulting in a deeper understanding of who Jesus is and what relationship with him means.

Desperation: What Miracles Are Made Of

Desperation isn't a popular state of being. No one wants to be the girl without a date for prom when all her friends have been asked, or the person sending a hundredth resume for jobs he or she really needs, or the guy on the corner with the sign that says "Anything will help."

Desperation isn't a preferred or pleasant condition, but it's the stuff that miracles are made of.

When I look closely at the miracle stories, I see a pattern. Right before each miracle, there is desperation: a person or group of people who are at the end of their ropes with no hope unless Jesus steps in to fix their situation.

Miracles are for desperate people. If you're not desperate, why would you need a miracle? In each miracle story, someone comes to the end of available choices—running out of ideas, options, strength, and resources—and Jesus steps in to make things right. Desperation always precedes a miracle.

I found that I had been so busy focusing on Jesus in these stories—perhaps the way one watches a magician carefully to figure out how he's doing the trick—that I had missed the other half of the equation completely: the someone that the miracle is for. And that someone is desperate.

Think about it: someone is blind or lame or dead. Someone's child is sick or dead or possessed by demons. Thousands of people are hungry, and there's not enough to feed them. A boat full of people is about to capsize. Ten people are walking around with leprosy, outcast from their families and community. A woman is bent over. A man's hand is withered beyond recognition. A woman has been bleeding for twelve years. Jesus is the miracle worker of those in despair, the Savior of desperate people.

Through the miracle stories, I discovered a new way of looking at God's glory. What if the glory of God is not just about the majestic, powerful acts that draw our attention but also about the specific people and situations God uses his power to help, which also cultivate our belief? This phenomenon of God's special attention for those at the bottom rung of society isn't limited to the miracle accounts. Again and again in Scripture, God turns the tables on our understanding of what it means to be blessed by God. When we say "I am so blessed," we usually mean a state of prosperity, health, and comfort. But reading the Sermon on the Mount turns this upside down.

In this amazing teaching in Matthew 5, Jesus rattles off a list of the types of people he sees as blessed, which we have come to call the Beatitudes. Instead of the prosperous and comfortable, we find a whole different kind of blessedness.

In God's economy, the poor in spirit, those in mourning, the meek, the persecuted, and those who are insulted and falsely accused are *blessed*. Even the celebrated "Blessed are the peacemakers" in verse 9, which is so often quoted from this list, means that those who are blessed to make peace are actually those who find themselves at the center of conflict, struggle, and war.

Why are these folks, whom we normally would view with pity, blessed? Because they know their need for God. Those of us who are still pretending we can get through life in our own strength don't often turn to God and ask for help. If God loves to bless the desperate, reach the broken, and heal those who come to him with their wounds, then the brokenness that causes us to cry out to him actually can be considered a blessing. The Beatitudes in their entirety can be summed up in the phrase *Blessed are the desperate, for they shall seek God and find him.*

Desperation is a gift from God because it teaches us we can't do life on our own. Every time we say to ourselves, "I can make it on my own," we are fooling ourselves, wearing a mask of self-reliance and believing a lie of self-subsistence. We're all, every one of us, badly in need of Jesus's help, but the truth is that it's only the desperate who go looking for it. And they are the ones who receive.

Desperation is the gift of not being able to pretend anymore. The hard things send us running into God's open arms. We see this gift of desperation in Jesus's first miracle when a bride's family runs out of wine. Before we unpack the desperation of the situation, let's consider how this miracle set the stage for Jesus's ministry and all of the miracles that would follow.

The Wedding at Cana

Jesus began his ministry of miracles at a wedding. The Gospel of John tells us that the changing of water into wine at a wedding near his hometown of Nazareth was the first of the signs Jesus performed. This was a new beginning for Jesus, and after this first sign nothing would be the same. John uses the word *sign* and not *miracle*. John is the only Gospel that never uses the word *miracle*. He always refers to Jesus's miraculous works as *signs*.

Think about the signs we read all day every day: the sign that marks the street where you're supposed to turn to get home, or the sign that points you toward the restrooms in a crowded shopping mall. If you are excited to see these signs, it's not because of the sign itself but because of where it points. Signs exist to call our attention to something more important, to act as the guide to what we are looking for.

Weddings are full of signs, the small, visible elements that point to a bigger reality that something incredibly important is going on. Two people walk down an aisle to meet each other, flanked by their closest friends and family. Rings, signifying an unbroken circle of love, are exchanged. Sometimes family members light two smaller candles that the couple uses to light a single candle together. Meaningful songs are sung, prayers are prayed, and vows are exchanged as promises of what is to come.

Most of all, these signs point to a new beginning. Two people walk into a room separately, but they leave together as one. This is the first day of a new life, a new start. After today, everything will be different.

Jesus used signs during this wedding miracle to drop hints about what

9

his own ministry would be. Since this was his first miracle, he packed it full of signs that point to his purpose and character. I read three signs in this miracle story.

1. Water

Water is a sign of new creation. In the very beginning of Genesis, "the Spirit of God was hovering over the waters" (1:2 NIV). Creation began with water, and John's Gospel takes us back to the beginning. John doesn't begin his Gospel with Jesus's birth but goes all the way back to echo the Creation story: "In the beginning was the Word, and the Word was with God, and the Word was God" (1:1). In the ministry of Jesus, God started all over again to restore the world to the newness of Eden.

Water is a sign of cleansing and purification. Water is what we call the universal solvent because it's able to dissolve more substances than any other liquid. When we wash our hands, our dishes, or our cars, we use water because it has the ability to surround and break down almost any impurity.

When Jesus asked the servants at the wedding to bring him some water, he did so in an incredibly specific way. In Jewish practice, coming near to God meant getting clean first. There were laws about impurity and how to get cleansed. Ritual washing was a way of seeking closeness to the Creator, and these jars were the containers meant for that purpose. Those at the party couldn't look at the jars without thinking about a ritual of physical washing that equaled spiritual purity.

Through Jesus's ministry, God turned the tables by being the One to bring spiritual cleansing to his people instead of waiting for them to clean themselves up before they could come close to him.

2. Wine

Wine is a sign of joy. The Jews had a saying: "Without wine, there is no joy."[1] Wine was a symbol of joy, and Jesus was bringing joy in overflowing abundance. A wedding party really needed more than a hundred gallons of wine, especially a wedding that had already run through their preplanned portion. So this sign of overflowing joy reminds us of Jesus's desire to give us more than just *enough* for our lives.

Compared with Moses, who turned water into blood as a sign of God's judgment (Exodus 7:14-24), Jesus changed ordinary water into wine as a sign of joy.

This may be a good time to mention that the association of wine and joy was not about drunkenness. Intoxication was considered a disgrace, and any mention of drunkenness in Scripture is associated with sin. In Jesus's day wine was the primary beverage for adults—safe to drink and somewhat more diluted than what we are used to today. So the mention of wine in abundance would not have meant drunkenness but joy. Joy is a response to abundance.

Wine is a sensory sign. Psalm 34:8 encourages us to "taste and see that the LORD is good." Scripture uses sensory language about God's goodness to help us remember that God is as real and tangible as the things we can taste, touch, and see with our senses. To paraphrase the verse, "May God be as real to you as the things right in front of your face." In other words, may God's goodness explode before your eyes with the joy of the face of your loved one or as the hot chocolate that hits your tongue. May you not only know about the love of God but also experience it deeply.

Wine is a sign of the Messiah. An abundance of wine is often used in the Old Testament to symbolize the blessings in the promised kingdom of God and the arrival of the Messiah. Thirst and dryness indicate that God's people are longing for the Messiah to come; while overflowing, dripping new wine is a signpost that the Messiah has come. In Isaiah 24 we find a dry and painful description of God's people and their situation. And then in chapter 25 we read of a banquet, held on a mountain, in celebration of the arrival of the Messiah. The wine and rich foods of the celebration point to other joys the Messiah will bring.

3. Weddings

The last sign is that of the wedding itself. Then, as now, weddings were occasions of great joy. Along with the Passover celebration, a wedding was the greatest day of celebration a community could experience.

Instead of being about only two people, a wedding is a gathering of an entire community to focus on love, hope, and unity. Weddings are not meant to be an exclusionary love of two people witnessed by bystanders. They are meant to point everyone present to the love of God.

Jesus chose the occasion of a wedding to show the power of God working through him for the first time. Throughout the Scriptures we see a connection between weddings and God's kingdom. One day we will finally and joyfully be fully united with God forever! Talk about abundant joy! Jesus started off his ministry with a wedding to say, "This is the beginning of something you have never seen before, and nothing will ever be the same again. I want to bring joy, purity, new creation, and an incredible oneness with you."

God wants us to look for signs, not in a demanding way—"God, give me a sign!"—but in a way of exploring the ever-signing God—"God has given me signs; what are they?" He wants us to look around and ask, "How is this sign, this event, this moment in time pointing me to You, Jesus?" The truth is, there are signs of God's love all around us every day, pointing us to Jesus.

Jesus's first miracle shows us that signs of God's love are everywhere. They are tangible and abundant. They are before us. Every single day we can taste and see that the Lord is good—including our most desperate moments.

Desperation at the Wedding

I remember well a moment of desperation at my wedding. The unity candle wouldn't light. You know, that symbol of two lives coming together as one. This tall candle stood on a high stand. We lifted our smaller candles up and tilted them down, and unwittingly just buried that little wick as we dripped hot wax on top of it. All the while we were hoping it would magically light, while all of our family and friends sat there and watched, thinking, "You know, it seems like a really bad omen if your unity candle won't light." I would have loved for that desperate moment to have preceded the miracle of light!

When you find yourself in a place where you run out of your own strength, that is precisely the place you may run into Jesus!

But where was the desperation at the wedding in Cana? A party was going on. They ran out of wine, and Jesus gave them a divine and abundant refill. Party on!

If we look at this miracle without understanding the backstory, it almost seems Jesus was performing a party trick for the disciples: "Hey guys! Look at this!" But we need to remember that this was a wedding in a first-century context, not a twenty-first-century context.

First of all, theirs was not a convenience culture—no sending someone running to the store for more to drink. Second, the wedding lasted a week or more, and wine was the main beverage for the guests. Finally, the social context in which this happened meant that it was no little faux pas but a major disaster.

Timothy Keller says, "This was not a mere breach of etiquette but a social and psychological catastrophe, particularly in a traditional honor-and-shame culture."[2] An honor-and-shame culture was one in which every social act brought either honor or shame to your family, your clan. Every individual represented a family, so any good or kind act from one individual to another meant there was a positive exchange, and the other family would owe them something in return (a reciprocal invitation or gift). A negative transaction, on the other hand, could bring shame that would last for generations.

A family essentially entered a social contract with other families when they invited them to a feast, promising to provide for their needs. So if they broke that contract by running out of wine, the groom and his family actually could be sued by the guests![3]

Here we have the most important event of a young couple's life. They were being introduced to life in the community that they would depend on for trade and commerce, support, social and religious community, and even future marriages of their children. If they were to get off on the wrong foot—and running out of wine is possibly the worst—they could be, at best, "the subject of this village's jests for years"[4] or, at worst, social pariahs cut off from the benefits of society in a day when all of a person's supplies for living came from community, not commerce.

The family was in a desperate situation, facing certain shame and guilt. Instead of a party trick, we see an introduction to what we will come to recognize as Jesus's specialty: using his power for the powerless and helpless to eliminate shame and guilt. Not only did he prevent certain disaster but he also turned a desperate situation into an abundant blessing.

Jesus not only turned the water into wine—he turned it into the *best* wine! And there was more than enough for everyone.

The place where the hosts ran out of wine is the place where they ran into Jesus, and it ended up being the best thing that could have happened. We will see this happen again and again in the miracle stories of Jesus as we look at the people in desperate need.

When we find ourselves in situations that could bring shame and guilt, we recognize that Jesus is the rescuer of desperate people. The only way to a deep connection with the powerful Christ of the miracles is first to encounter our deep need for him. If we think we can enjoy his power without first admitting our own powerlessness, we are mistaken. When we find ourselves in a place where we run out of our own strength, that is precisely the place we may run into Jesus!

Mary Recognizes the Desperate Need

At the heart of the story of Jesus turning water into wine during a wedding at Cana is a conversation between Jesus and his mother, Mary. This dialogue may be one of the most misunderstood in the Bible, since so many people read it without taking time to understand Jesus and Mary inside and out, both their world and their hearts.

If we read the conversation between Jesus and his mother through our own cultural lens, we may end up a little shocked. Mary could seem bossy and unrelenting. Jesus could sound resentful and adolescent. One might wonder how the Son of God could speak to his own mother in such a tone—the same tone I might refer to when telling my kids, "Don't take that *tone* with me!"

Today's cultural understanding might lead us to hear Mary's statement with the same tone a mother might use to say, "Your socks are in the middle of the floor." It's a statement that's not really a statement but a passive-aggressive request or demand.

But wine had a much deeper significance in their culture. You'll remember that it was a sign of joy because it signified the coming of the Messiah. If wine was a sign that God was showing up in power and love to save his people, imagine what the absence of wine would mean.

Isaiah 24:7-11 depicts a hurting nation longing for God to send the Messiah, the One who will come and save them. A dry and thirsty people—merrymakers who had run out of wine—would signify that people were longing, thirsty, and ready for God to come and save them. So at the wedding in Cana, when Mary said, "They have no wine," she was essentially saying, "Look, Jesus. They are longing for the Messiah!" (John 2:3). What a beautiful sign of God's people being ready to receive him.

As a mother—and one who had received miraculous messages about her son before he was ever born—Mary had kept a close eye on Jesus his entire life. Lately she had seen his ministry emerging: his baptism by his cousin John and his calling of disciples to follow him. Now she was likely wondering if this sign, the wine running out, meant that it was time for Jesus to step into a more public role.

It's a gift to admit failure, want, and lack, because ultimately it brings us to rely on God's help. Mary was the only one willing to point out the desperate situation at this wedding. This story is a beautiful picture of a people in need of help being connected with the One who has the power to help them, not only with their need for wine but also with their need for God's intervention in their lives. Mary is a hero in this story, not a nag.

Our cultural understanding today might leave us shocked by what we perceive as the blatant disrespect in Jesus's words. Picture yourself addressing your own mother or a woman in a position of authority as "*Woman*"! "Woman, make me dinner!" "Woman, what are you talking about?" That kind of talk would not go over well in my family and probably not in yours either. But in Jesus's culture, addressing someone with the word *woman* was a sign of respect—similar to someone today calling a woman "ma'am."

When Mary brought up Jesus's messiahship by referring to the lack of wine, he reminded her that his hour had not yet come. When *would* his hour come? To answer that, we must go to the garden of Gethsemane, the final hour when mercy and sacrifice flow liberally would involve the death and resurrection of Jesus. Jesus knew that the thirst for Messiah, echoed in the thirst for wine, would be answered only in his own death and resurrection. He wasn't speaking of "the hour" as the start of his ministry but as the final culmination. In that final hour, Jesus would set in motion the beginning of the greatest miracle of all time—his resurrection. That hour would hold within it fear, forgiveness, trust, surrender, and obedience. And as we see from this first miracle to the last, obedience was an essential ingredient.

The Essential Ingredient of Obedience

We are drawn to the miracle stories because of the power of an omnipotent God on display in his mighty acts. But in addition to his power, there is a quieter character on display in the miracles: our obedience.

Think about the servants at the wedding banquet. This celebration was obviously a huge workload for them. Feeding and serving all of these additional guests for a multiple-day—possibly multiple-week—party meant that they had been working overtime to provide for the needs of the guests. They were probably the first ones to notice that the wine had run out, and they may have felt anxious that they would be blamed when the next guest ordered a refill and they had to tell them there was no wine. One thing was certain: wine is not something that could be manufactured or made quickly.

Then one of the party guests pointed to her son and spoke those iconic words: "Do whatever he tells you" (John 2:5). This statement is the blank check of obedience. Who knew what this new teacher would command? When he did speak, it certainly was out of the ordinary.

I can only imagine the stressed expressions of the servants as they anticipated the angry look on the face of the master of the banquet when they dipped a cup for tasting into a jar they had just filled with water. Perhaps when things went wrong, it was the servants who took the blame—and sometimes the beating. For whatever reason, they were willing to obey the stranger's odd instructions.

The servants discovered that obedience isn't easy work. They obeyed fully, hauling enough water to fill six large jars. No slacking; no room for doubt that someone had added anything other than water to the jars.

Because of their obedience, the servants had a front-row seat to God's power on display. The steward or master was confused when he drank the wine, not knowing where it came from, and the others at the party might have drawn their own conclusions about when and how the new and improved wine appeared. But the servants saw the miracle in action. They knew the truth. In a way, Jesus was actually giving the servants something that not even the honored guests or even the master of the party knew: they were receiving firsthand knowledge of Jesus's power. Though this is the first miracle that Jesus performed publicly, it's not very public because only the servants are let in on the secret.

It's amazing how often obedience is an essential ingredient of a miracle. Finding the small acts of human obedience that are a part of God's miracles may not always be as exciting as looking for the mind-blowing results of God's actions, but it shows us how he loves to work in relationship with his people. Let's look at a few examples together.

God never simply said, "Hey, Moses, watch this." Instead he told him to stretch out his hand to part the Red Sea, strike a rock with his staff to produce water, and raise his staff in the air to be victorious in battle. God often uses some gift or resource we already possess as the catalyst for a miracle when we put what is in our hands in his hands.

Naaman, who sought healing from God for a terrible and isolating skin disease, is another example. In his desperation, he even traveled to another nation to find a prophet who could tell him what to do. But he balked when the instructions included dipping himself seven times in an "inferior" river. Only when Naaman was obedient, doing something he considered beneath him, did his healing occur (2 Kings 5:1-14).

God is always on the side of restoration and wholeness, but he calls us to participate in our own healing by obeying him. Our internal lives often need as much or more healing than our bodies, and obedience to God many times brings healing to both.

In the miracle stories, an act of obedience is often required for a miraculous outcome. God calls us to act in faith, trusting that he will meet our needs. And prayer is generally a part of this process. In fact, prayer is obedience. Those who pray in desperation and then see God's answers unfold have a front-row seat to God at work, while others may tend to view amazing outcomes as coincidence. Mary certainly had a front-row seat to God's miraculous power.

It's no accident that Mary was the one who instructed the servants to do whatever Jesus told them to do. Her own story is a witness to the miracles that often follow obedience.

While Mary was still an unmarried teenage girl, an angel told her that she would become pregnant and give birth to the Son of God. Though she wondered how this would be accomplished, since she was a virgin, her response was one of obedience: "May it be done to me according to your word" (Luke 1:38 NASB).

Contrast Mary's example to that of her relative's husband, Zechariah. While Mary was of low status—female, young, unmarried, and poor—Zechariah was of high status—male, older, married, and of the priestly class. Yet when told in a similar manner that his aging and barren wife, Elizabeth, would have a son (John the Baptist), Zechariah responded differently. Zechariah was struck mute until his son was born, but Mary was blessed with affirmation when she went to visit Elizabeth (Luke 1).

Mary is known as an icon of obedience, for she not only gave birth to Jesus "according to [God's] word" but also raised him and witnessed his death and resurrection. It's no wonder she identified with the servants at the wedding in Cana and reminded them to "do whatever he tells you." She lived by those words, being obedient to God.

A life of full obedience is what God desires from each of us. It won't always be easy, but it is always our best choice.

Here's the thing about recognizing the relationship between our obedience and God's miracles: it keeps us dependent on God. Rather than the kind of white-knuckled, teeth-gritted determination that results from believing that we obey God by acting alone and in our strength, we see our actions as part of God's work, remembering that his power is at work in and through us. By obeying God, we are playing a part in his grander plan. It also keeps us from becoming detached spectators of God's work in the world.

If we approach miracles thinking God will knock our socks off by doing all the work himself, we miss the point. God wants to involve each of us in the plan for his kingdom to come here on earth as it is in heaven. If you would like a front-row seat to see God at work and be part of the amazing transformation of the world we live in, put on a servant's uniform and "do whatever he tells you."

Your desperation is a gift if you'll allow it to be. Don't try to hide the places of your weakness, dryness, or running out. Instead of running from these things, lean into them. This is where you're going to meet Jesus. Your best will always run out. His best will always be better. Your desperation will lead you to ask for a tiny refill, but he will bypass the bottles you have emptied and say instead, "Bring me the jars and fill them to the top with 150 gallons of grace." Grace upon grace upon grace.

CHAPTER 2

THE MIRACLE OF ABUNDANCE

FROM OUR LITTLE, JESUS MAKES MUCH

God loves to deal in the small. I know that sounds like a contradiction in a study about miracles, where we step back in awe of the big and bold actions of God, but it's true. The big things that God does often begin with something small.

When our family moved to Kentucky, Jim and I decided to bring four-year-old Drew along on the house-hunting trip with us to help him through the transition of moving to a new place. As four-year-olds sometimes do, Drew decided that he was along on the trip not for his benefit but for *ours* and that his opinion was needed in the process of searching for a new house. In his little mind he had developed his own list of must-haves: a fireplace, a basement (since he had never even seen one while living in Texas), and a garden. In the small town to which we were moving, our Realtor only found four houses to show us that were in our price range. In each, Drew would announce "No fireplace!" or name some other way in which the house didn't fit his qualifications, and that would be that. To be honest, none of the four seemed to Jim and me to be the home that would best suit our family's needs. Discouraged and tired, we called it quits for the day.

Just as we were about to give up, a family friend who lived in town happened to mention that she knew someone who was planning to sell their home but had not yet put it on the market. A phone call was made, and before we knew it we were standing on the doorstep of a home that certainly looked made just for us. As we walked from room to room, my heart soared as I dreamed of how this would be the perfect place for our family. I was so lost in thought that I barely heard Drew ticking off the things on his little list as he saw them: "Fireplace!" "Basement!" And then, as we finished the tour of the inside and were shown the perfect backyard for Drew and his sister to play in, the homeowner happened to mention that she recently had started a small garden off to the side. I thought my son would combust with joy! We had found our home. As tiny as these details seem, it was the small things that God used to guide us to the house we now call home—and even to meet the requests of a little boy looking for his heart's desires.

Throughout Scripture we find small things popping up again and again that signal God's attention to detail. Little David conquers Goliath with just a small stone (1 Samuel 17:48-50). A minuscule cloud signifies the beginning of a great storm the prophet Elijah predicted (1 Kings 18:41-46). Elijah hears God in the sound of sheer silence, not the earthquake, fire, or wind (1 Kings 19:11-13). Jesus points to a tiny mustard seed as the representation of true faith, since it starts out small but grows large (Matthew 13:31-32). James indicates that the tongue is powerful and mighty, reminding us that "a small spark" can ignite a forest fire (James 3:5 NIV).

A scarcity of ingredients reminds us that it's God's power, not human ingenuity or provision, to which we should give our attention and praise. The harder the odds and the smaller the resources, the more amazed we are when God comes through and makes something amazing out of almost nothing.

No miracle exemplifies this quite as well as the day Jesus fed a crowd of five thousand.

Feeding Five Thousand

As the narrative begins in Mark 6, we discover the disciples are tired and worn out from ministering to others, and they've been so busy they haven't even had a chance to eat (vv. 30-31). I'm sure you've felt like this from time to time, when your responsibilities and care for others have drained you so much that you are desperately in need of time just to care for yourself.

Jesus invites the disciples to come to a quiet place where they can rest. They cross over to the other side of the lake in a boat, but people hurry by foot to get there ahead of them, so that when they arrive another great crowd has already formed (v. 33). This helps us understand the crowds that are gathering around Jesus during his ministry, especially around the Sea of Galilee. This is not a very large region, and the towns are not very far apart. So when people witness the amazing things Jesus is doing, they tell their friends and rush ahead to the next town where they can find him.

When Jesus, who is still tired and hungry from his ministry in the previous town, arrives, he encounters a brand-new crowd—described as "great" in size. Here's the story's first mention of scarcity. Jesus notices first that they are starving for leadership, teaching, and truth, so he "[begins] to teach them many things" (v. 34). Then, at the end of a long day of teaching, the disciples call Jesus's attention to another kind of scarcity in the situation.

The disciples are exhausted and hungry, the crowds are "great" in size but lack a shepherd to care for them, and now we find that thousands of people are also hungry. When Jesus tells the disciples to take inventory, they find themselves digging in their pockets for crumbs! John's Gospel tells us that another of Jesus's disciples, Andrew, who is Simon Peter's brother, speaks up after searching the crowd for any food. You can hear the exasperation in his voice: "Here is a boy with five small barley loaves and two small fish, but how far will they go among so many?" (6:8-9 NIV).

Just because miracles are impossible to understand doesn't mean they have to be impossible to believe.

It seems a bit strange to complain to a limitless God about how impossible your situation is, but that's what the disciples are doing here. In fact, our prayers sometimes sound this way too; we lay our desperate situations out before the King of kings and tell him just how impossible things look to us.

But there's a small detail in this miracle story that we don't want to miss. I call it a *small* detail because we're talking here about things that are small in our eyes but great in Jesus's hands. The detail is, of course, the boy. It's not a disciple who provides the small offering with which Jesus will make a miracle. It's not even an adult. It's a boy. Don't miss this: the disciples aren't the ones in the story with the resources. They are totally out of food, out of ideas, and out of patience, wanting Jesus to just send everybody home so they can be done. They have nothing to offer. But the boy does.

The disciple who acts as the go-between, bringing the boy and his food to Jesus, is Andrew. Otherwise, this little one and his gifts might have been lost in the crowd. I have a personal love for the disciple Andrew because we named our son, our firstborn, Andrew. (He goes by Drew, he'll proudly tell you.)

Andrew shows remarkable humility and wisdom in the story of the feeding of the five thousand. He knows he could be laughed at when he presents a small boy with a tiny lunch to Jesus. But despite his own question regarding the sufficiency of that small amount, he must also know that any offering, no matter how small, is something great in Jesus's hands.

When we put our small resources in God's hands, they are more than enough. When blessed in Jesus's hands, the five loaves and two fish turned out to be a feast for a multitude. Jesus actually divided five loaves among everyone, and then amazingly he divided the two fish among all of them too.

The result is mind-blowing. We're told not only that everyone ate but also that *all* were satisfied! And to show that God is more than enough for all our needs, the disciples took up leftovers and filled twelve baskets!

Don't miss the number: twelve. Remember our tired and weary disciples? There were twelve of them. The number of leftover baskets helped to remind them that just as they took care of the needs of others—distributing the food and giving them something to eat—God would always take care of their needs as well.

If you are concerned or worried about someone in your life, bring the person to Jesus. Pray for him or her. Even that tiny act is enough for something great.

Just as in the miracle at the wedding in Cana, when there was a need to refill wine bottles and the result was an overflow of wine in large stone jars, God is always "able to do immeasurably more than all we ask or imagine" (Ephesians 3:20 NIV).

There are people who analyze this miracle in a way that implies that it is no miracle at all, saying that the people just reached into their coats for the little bit of food they brought and, inspired by Jesus, began sharing generously. While generosity is indeed a gift, this text, told in all four Gospels, clearly gives us a glimpse of the awe that both the crowd and the disciples had at Jesus's miraculous actions. Just because miracles are impossible to understand doesn't mean they have to be impossible to believe. Miracles are an opportunity to marvel at the marvelous, not to explain away the unexplainable.

The crowd was large. The hunger and exhaustion were great. The boy was small. The five loaves and two fish were small. *But Jesus is enough!*

Stuart Briscoe reminds us that "human resources, however limited, when willingly offered and divinely empowered, are more than adequate to achieve divine ends."[1] Remember that what is small in our hands is big in Jesus's hands. Wait with expectancy, and just see what great things he can do! Oftentimes we just have to take that first step and admit that the situation is desperate.

Admitting Our Desperation

Have you ever been part of a group that is invited to publicly share their prayer requests? Some Bible study groups, Sunday school classes, and even worship gatherings have a period when they open the floor and invite people to share their concerns and joys in prayer. While this can be an incredibly beautiful time of sharing needs and offering promises to pray, it can also make some people feel incredibly uncomfortable.

To tell the truth, most of us don't like to share our most vulnerable needs with others. We are sometimes afraid that it will make us seem weak or helpless to admit that we don't have our lives under control and that there are things we desperately need help, even the Lord's help, solving.

Sometimes, as I sit in a circle of people who are sharing prayer requests, I am thinking to myself, "Which of my needs should I share and ask for prayer about? Definitely not _____ (my most vulnerable area) but also not _____ (something trivial). Maybe I'll ask them to pray for _____ (something in the middle)." Aren't we humans ridiculous in our posturing to make sure we look good in each other's eyes?

Desperation is the element that breaks down our posturing. Being desperate means we know we need something that is a necessity for our lives yet is completely out of our control. In the prayer request circle, this usually begins with issues related to health. Struggles with our own health or concerns about the health of those we love are at the top of the list of things we cannot control yet want desperately to see resolved. That is why many of our initial steps of trust in sharing prayer requests begin with comments such as, "Please pray for my uncle who had a stroke," or "Pray for my medical tests this week." This is a wonderful place for us to start trusting the Lord and each other with our needs, and we'll see in coming chapters that Jesus often addressed people's deep concerns about their own health and the health of their loved ones through miracles of healing, casting out evil spirits, and raising the dead.

Another level of trust in many groups is often sharing prayer requests for help with provision. This often involves requests for those searching for a new job, those concerned about discord or instability at work, or those with unexpected or overwhelming bills who are trying to make ends meet. This is another wonderful area to recognize our need before God, since all that we are and all that we have comes from him. We tend to forget this until there is a moment when our physical needs are in danger of not being met, and then we remember to turn to him for provision for our bellies, our bills, and our bank accounts.

The most powerful prayers I've prayed in my life usually have been in community with others. When I pray alone, a little trickle of desperation is sent God's way; but when I join my prayer with the tributaries of the prayers of others, a rushing river of petitions flows to the throne of God. It's in small groups of friends that I've really learned to pray, listening to the sometimes faltering, sometimes powerful, words of those around me. I can think of times when I've taken a risk to say out loud a deep need of my heart and then heard the voice of a dear friend repeating that need in prayer to God. An unbelievable freedom has rushed through me at those times, knowing that I am loved and supported—not alone in my needs and prayers.

As we move into deeper levels of trust with God and with one another, we realize that Jesus, who is the bread of life, is the One responsible for filling all our needs. He reminds us of this in John 6 when he tells the disciples, "I am the bread of life. Whoever comes to me will never go hungry, and whoever believes in me will never be thirsty" (John 6:35 NIV).

Having just witnessed the miracle of the feeding of the five thousand, the disciples seem very focused on physical hunger and fullness. Jesus calls them out on this, saying, "Very truly I tell you, you are looking for me, not because you saw the signs I performed but because you ate the loaves and had your fill" (John 6:26 NIV). And in the next verse, he invites them to think about spiritual hunger: "Do not work for food that spoils, but for food that endures to eternal life" (v. 27 NIV).

Jesus's teaching goes all the way back to the forty years that their ancestors spent wandering in the wilderness and the bread that God gave them there called *manna*, which simply means "What is it?"

In the wilderness God provided for the Israelites' needs out of nothing; the bread simply materialized from thin air each morning. This is not unlike the nothingness the disciples encounter on the hillside with five thousand hungry people wanting bread. Mark tells us in his Gospel that Jesus asks them to take inventory of their scarcity: "'How many loaves do you have?' he asked. 'Go and see'" (Mark 6:38 NIV). They come up with next to nothing, but when they know exactly how much nothing they have, that's where Jesus's everything begins.

After the miracle, the people find Jesus on the other side of the lake and ask for this miraculous, life-giving, never-running-out bread. Jesus responds by offering himself—the true bread of life. Those who come to him will never be hungry or thirsty.

God provides for all of our needs. We can't always figure out how he will do it. We don't always understand his methods. But he will always be there to meet our needs. God always provides.

One of the most amazing parts of this miracle of providing bread and the teaching on the bread of life that follows it is that Jesus understands our hunger. He has already been faced with the same lesson the disciples are facing—the same one the Israelites in the wilderness faced—and he demonstrated trust in the provision of God. Jesus himself has been hungry and wanted bread. He himself was given the choice of trusting God for his provision or taking shortcuts that would mean certain physical satisfaction but spiritual failure.

At the very beginning of his ministry, immediately following his baptism, Jesus went to the wilderness to be tempted by Satan. Alone in the wilderness for forty days, Jesus was hungry—not just I-skipped-breakfast hungry but I-could-eat-an-elephant-and-then-order-seconds hungry. He had been fasting forty days, and we're told that at the end of that time Satan came to tempt him to fill his belly. This tells us something about the times when we are most vulnerable to temptation. Times when we are hungry or lonely or tired are often the moments when our character is tested most.

The first temptation Satan used to challenge Jesus had to do with hunger.

Jesus had the need for bread and the power to make bread, yet he didn't use his power to satisfy himself. He knew that divine power was not a commodity to be used as if God's purpose is always to answer our whims. Jesus's miracles would reveal his self-giving nature, intended to satisfy others' needs, not his own.

When Jesus was faced with temptation, he recalled the Israelites' desert journey and remembered God's faithfulness even when they were not faithful. This is great news for us when we are tempted and fail: Jesus came to be the faithful answer to the challenges we face.

If you find yourself tempted, tested, and tried, stop and ask Jesus for help. He has been tempted in every way we can be, yet he resisted them all (Hebrews 4:15). We can trust in his goodness, faithfulness, and love.

Jesus's resistance to the temptation to create bread for his own physical hunger reveals that he would not use his power at a whim to impress others, or even feed himself, but he would use his power to meet people's deepest needs and fulfill God's purposes on earth. He denied himself for others. This self-denying love showed up throughout his ministry. From his wilderness temptations that launched his active ministry on earth to his death on the cross that ended it, he trusted in God's provision. He knew that his Father would provide.

Mark Buchanan, a popular author and pastor, says that although many people over the years have asked for his prayers when they were facing bankruptcy and financial ruin, not one person has ever asked him to pray with them over how to invest their money. We often think of asking God for help when all of our human wisdom and resources are at an end, but we rarely realize that God wants to be intimately involved in all steps of the provision for our lives.[2]

How about you? Do you wait until desperation has you in its clutches before you realize God is right there, eager to be part of your needs, your abundance, and every aspect of your life? When we are faithful to look to him, he will always provide.

The Four-Gospel Miracle

The feeding of the five thousand is the only miracle of Jesus other than the resurrection told in all four Gospels.

In case you missed the importance of that statement, let me say it in a different way: Of all the stories told about Jesus's miracles, the feeding of the five thousand is the only one that was retold by all four Gospel writers. James Martin says that simple fact is actually a gigantic indicator "that provides a gauge for how dramatic, memorable, and important [this] event was for the disciples and the early church."[3]

Each of the Gospel writers gives us details that set the scene for this miracle. Matthew gives us a concise account of Jesus going away to a deserted place and the crowds following him. Mark gives the same details but adds that Jesus took the disciples along too. Mark is the most detailed and action-packed account, with lots of action verbs thrown in. While Luke sticks with the facts, he tells us that Jesus was in the region of Bethsaida, a name that means "house of fish"[4]—highlighting the fish that would be part of the meal to come. John includes the element of timing, telling us that it was the time of Passover. This detail makes it even richer when we see the disciples sharing a meal together, as Jews did at Passover to mark the freedom given them in the Exodus. John is always calling our attention to symbols that will be the signs pointing to different aspects of Jesus's ministry, and this sign helps us see the freedom Jesus wants to bring to God's people the way Moses brought freedom to the Israelites.

Mark also is the one who connects for us the setting of green grass (mentioned in more than one account), Jesus's vision of the people as sheep without a shepherd, and the command for people to "recline"—showing a banquet. These details have echoes of Psalm 23: "The LORD is my shepherd.... He makes me lie down in green pastures."

Even the way the various Gospels provide a setting for the story shows us how a different viewpoint can call our attention to different aspects of the message.

The four accounts also paint for us a picture of the problem, each bringing a different nuance or emphasis just as four persons retelling the same story would do. Matthew again presents the basic facts of the situation: the place was isolated, the hour was late, and the disciples suggested sending the people away. Mark expands on those facts and hints at an emotional urgency in his tone by emphasizing how late it was and the amount of money that would be necessary to buy bread. Luke adds the practical detail of lodging, noting that the people should also look for a place to stay. John shows more individual conversation between the disciples, emphasizing Philip's practicality and then telling how Andrew brought the boy forward with the resources that would provide a solution.

Every Gospel indicates how desperate the situation of encountering a hungry crowd can be, but each one emphasizes a different aspect of the conditions we find there.

As different as the accounts are, they suddenly converge and come to almost surprising accuracy in agreement about the details of exactly how Jesus handled the meal in this story.

- Through the disciples, Jesus commanded the people to sit.
- Jesus took the bread.

- Jesus looked up to heaven.
- Jesus blessed/gave thanks.
- Jesus broke/divided the elements. (John is the only one who doesn't indicate that Jesus broke the elements.)
- Jesus distributed the elements through the disciples.

This tight consistency in the set of events indicates a desire to tell the story in a way that mirrors closely the Lord's Supper, which we will consider again in a later chapter. Although the feeding of the five thousand occurred before the Last Supper, which happened on the night before Jesus's death, we must remember that the authors were writing their Gospels *after* Jesus's death and resurrection. They would have recognized the similarities between the actions on that hillside and the actions in the upper room, and they would have wanted people reading to see them as well.

All four Gospel accounts proclaim the same outcome—that the whole crowd was filled. This wasn't just the edge being taken off their hunger; they were satisfied! And there was enough for leftovers, filling twelve baskets. In John's Gospel, people reacted by comparing Jesus to a prophet. All of the accounts also agree that once the crowds were fed, Jesus went on his way up the mountain to be alone; however, only John mentions that the crowd was pursuing and trying to make him king (John 6:15). It becomes clear that the way the story starts, with Jesus longing to have some time alone for prayer and rest, is the way the story ends—with his wishes being fulfilled.

For some, reading the different accounts of Jesus's life in the four Gospels causes confusion or doubt. They wonder: Why do we have four stories of Jesus's life? How do four different accounts of the same story have four different sets of details? Others have speculated that the stories contradict one another and should cause us to doubt the accuracy of the accounts.

But the differences in the ways the Gospel writers tell the stories actually *add* to their credibility, not detract from it. They are doing their job according to their own first-century culture, not according to ours in the twenty-first century.

Many biblical scholars have warned us not to read the Gospels as if they are modern biographies. Our modern biographers are expected to be impartial, detached observers, writing down what we'd call "just the facts"—and as many facts, dates, and details as possible. But in the time the Gospels were written, it was entirely acceptable—and even expected— that the Gospel writers were interpreting the facts as they went, using the *way* they wrote the story to get across the points they wanted us to hear. It was expected that they would change the order of the sequence of events or emphasize or leave out a detail if it meant getting their theological point across to their intended audience.[5]

So, rather than be bothered by the differences you see in different accounts of the miracle stories, be a curious observer of the details. As you read, ask God, "How can what I am reading help me grow in my relation- ship to You?" And always remember that whenever you read God's Word, you are holding a treasure in your hands, the very breath of God—for "all Scripture is God-breathed and is useful for teaching, rebuking, correcting and training in righteousness, so that the servant of God may be thoroughly equipped for every good work" (2 Timothy 3:16-17 NIV). God uses every little detail in Scripture to point you to him, and one story echoes back to another that echoes back to another, all pointing to an abundantly gener- ous God who is who he says he is.

Echoes of Abundance

We use stories to tell stories all the time. If you're hearing a tale described as "a real Cinderella story," you immediately know that it's about someone rising from a low position to shine in prominence. A tax described as a "Robin Hood" tax makes you think of a story where someone takes from the rich to give to the poor. Describe someone as a "Scrooge," a "Don Juan," or a bit of a "Jekyll and Hyde" (or even a "Judas"), and you're using a literary allusion to a story to explain what you mean about the story you are telling.

Stories are often used to illuminate stories. When people experienced or heard the story of Jesus feeding the multitude, what other events did it bring to mind? There are allusions scattered throughout the story of Jesus feeding thousands on the hillside that immediately would have brought other events to mind for the hearers, and those echoes would have given them some clue about God and his larger story—clues that we might miss unless we delve into the background of some of these events.

What can we learn about the story of the feeding of the five thousand if we examine the stories hidden within the story? The Gospel writers wanted this story to feel very familiar, bringing up the memories of how faithful God had been to them in past situations. The story of the feeding of the five thousand highlights that God's saving acts through miraculous means have been going on for a long time. It tells us that God is faithful and can be trusted. When we dig under the surface of this miracle account, we unearth some wonderful references to God's abundant provision, power, compassion, and faithfulness throughout Scripture.

Moses and Passover

One story within this miracle story of the feeding of the five thousand has to do with Moses leading God's people to freedom through the wilderness. As we learned earlier, John seems to give a random detail in his Gospel account of this miracle without elaboration or explanation, noting that it was near the time of the Passover (John 6:4). Though we briefly considered this detail earlier, let's take another look.

Each year during the Passover feast, God's people remembered and rehearsed the story of God's faithfulness in their escape from slavery in Egypt. During the meal, they remembered the wilderness wanderings and the miraculous ways God provided abundantly for his hungry and thirsty people by bringing the miracles of water, quail, and manna—bread provided from heaven new every morning (see Exodus 16). The crowd of hungry people who are fed abundantly by Jesus soon will be celebrating the Passover, which commemorates God's abundant provision.

In John 6:25-59 we read that the very next day a crowd hears about the miraculous feeding, goes to find Jesus, and engages in conversation with him, wondering if he's a kind of new Moses because he has brought them bread. This intriguing conversation culminates with Jesus making an astounding promise: "I am the bread of life. Whoever comes to me will never be hungry, and whoever believes in me will never be thirsty" (v. 35).

Instead of just another prophet bringing bread that will be eaten up, Jesus proclaims that he himself *is* the bread of life! This statement simultaneously points back to the Exodus—indicating God is about to free his people from slavery—and points forward to the Last Supper and the cross.

Elijah and the Widow

The feeding of the five thousand also echoes one of the greatest stories of abundance found in Scripture: the encounter of the prophet Elijah and the widow of Zarephath, told in 1 Kings 17. This woman was at such a point of desperation when she met the prophet that she was in the process of gathering a few sticks to cook what she thought was her last meal. Even more heartbreaking she had a son, whom she thought would die of starvation along with her.

Elijah comforted her by telling her not to be afraid, promising that God would take care of her and her son until the severe drought of her country ended, but first he asked her to do something unheard of. She only had enough for one last meal, and a complete stranger was asking that she make him a loaf of bread first! Can you imagine!

In an act of faith that we may not be able to comprehend, the widow faithfully followed his instruction. What a beautiful parallel to the faith of the little boy in the crowd who, instead of hoarding his resources, offered them to Jesus and saw them multiply beyond his wildest dreams.

I love the picture of abundance that follows in Elijah's story. Each time the widow dipped into the flour, there was enough. Each time she poured oil out of the jug, there was enough, and that happened again and again until the drought and famine passed. This must have taken a daily act of faith on her part—first to give her "last loaf" to the prophet, and then to go to her pantry day after day and find that God provided, literally, her daily bread.

Another story of abundance within the miracle story of the feeding of the five thousand has to do with the prophet Elisha. The stories of the prophet Elijah and his protégé, the younger prophet Elisha, are favorites of mine. In my study *Set Apart: Holy Habits of Prophets and Kings*, I talk about how Elisha asked God for a double portion of the spirit of his mentor Elijah once the elder man was gone. Indeed, if you follow Elisha's ministry, many of his miracles are echoes of Elijah's earlier miracles, and (depending on how you count) he did perform double the number of miracles of Elijah.

Elijah's encounter with the widow of Zarephath, when God multiplied the flour and oil for her and her son, is echoed in a later miracle that Elisha performed. Second Kings 4:1-7 tells us that yet another widow was in a desperate situation in which her creditors were about to take her sons as slaves if she could not pay her debts. Elisha asked her "What do you have in your house?" (v. 2 NIV), and she mentioned a small jar of olive oil. He instructed her to borrow all the empty bottles and jars she could from her neighbors and begin pouring the small jar of oil into each of them. When she did, she found that the small jar kept pouring and pouring! Finally, when the last borrowed jar was filled, the oil stopped. She sold the oil and paid her debts, and once again God multiplied another tiny resource into a big solution.

But yet another of Elisha's miracles bears even closer resemblance to Jesus's miracle of feeding five thousand. Barley loaves—which were small, rustic loaves of bread—were the food of the poor. Any of God's people listening to Jesus's story and hearing about the barley loaves would immediately think of Elisha's story and be amazed by the greater numbers that

Jesus fed. The main echo would be the abundance of God that resounds throughout Scripture.

The Last Supper

The last story within a story found in the feeding of five thousand is not an echo backward in time but a foreshadowing of what is to come at the Last Supper in the upper room. The acts of taking the loaves, blessing them, breaking them, and giving them to his disciples echo Jesus's actions at the Last Supper as he offers the bread and cup to his disciples. Don't miss the significance of the similarities. These parallels let us know that the miracle of miraculous multiplication didn't end on that day on the hillside. We are included *every* time we participate in the blessing, breaking, and offering of bread and wine. Jesus is the bread of life, and he came to satisfy the deep needs of the world—the deep needs of you and me. The abundance of that day is evidence of God's desire to abundantly provide for our needs today.

God's abundance is greater than you ever imagined. I'm reminded of Paul's words to the Philippians, which are still true today for each one of us: "And my God will meet all your needs according to the riches of his glory in Christ Jesus" (Philippians 4:19 NIV). On that hillside, Jesus sat among a crowd and met an immediate need that would point to a spiritual need. He brought about food in abundance in a desperate situation. The crowd would repeatedly press in around Jesus, one time even forcing him to hop in a fishing boat to create some distance, setting the scene for a life-changing encounter with Simon Peter.

An Abundant Catch

Remember making wish lists as a kid? When it came time for Christmas or your birthday, did you write a list of everything you could possibly want? Or did you circle items and dog-ear pages in a catalog? I remember going through the many catalogs we would get in the mail (my mom was a teacher, so we got some great ones!), circling items and leaving subtle notes like "I really want this!" and then leaving them carefully placed on the coffee table, hoping my mom would get the hint.

The disciple Simon Peter experienced a fulfillment of his wish list that meant success beyond his dreams, but his response may be surprising.

Let me set the scene. We're at the beginning of Jesus's ministry. According to the ordering of events in Luke's Gospel, here is what happens:

- Jesus is baptized by John the Baptist. (3:21)
- Jesus is tempted by Satan during his forty-day fast in the wilderness. (4:1-13)
- Jesus preaches a sermon that gets him thrown out of his hometown synagogue in Nazareth. (4:14-29)
- Jesus travels to the towns surrounding the Sea of Galilee and begins doing things that astonish people: he casts an evil spirit out of a man and goes to Simon Peter's house where he heals Peter's mother-in-law of a fever. (4:31-38)
- Now people are bringing those who are sick and demon possessed to Jesus, and he is healing them. (4:40-41)

Crowds of people are starting to gather. They love listening to Jesus and are amazed at his teaching, because he speaks with authority (4:32), as well as the power and authority with which he commands demons and heals people (v. 36). The more miracles Jesus performs in public, the more the crowds come.

In Luke 5 Jesus is teaching the crowds on the shore of Galilee one day, and they're crowding him to the very edge. Jesus looks out and sees two boats and an opportunity. He calls them over and uses one of the boats as a floating pulpit to teach the crowds, which was an ingenious solution to being able to be near enough to teach but not so close that the crowds push against him while he does it. Then Jesus turns to Peter, the owner of the particular boat he's in, and gives an unusual order. The order is directed straight at Peter. Even though there are other fishermen present, this story is told with a spotlight on Peter because it's a one-on-one conversation. Of all the fisherman in the boats, only Peter speaks to Jesus. And when Jesus speaks, he addresses only Peter, using singular verbs: "Don't be afraid; from now on you will fish for people" (v. 10 NIV).

It's common for us to feel unworthy in the presence of the divine, but God always answers with the assurance that it is not our worthiness that counts.

Consider what's probably going through Peter's mind. He's tired and skeptical. It's dubious that this carpenter from a neighboring town can just jump in a boat and seem to know Peter's trade better than he does. It's clear that they've been out all night (a typical time for fishing); they have tried every trick they know as professionals and have come up empty. It would be easy for Peter to refuse. Jesus has already asked the favor of using the boat to teach from; isn't that enough? But two things push Peter to trust Jesus enough to give it a try: (1) Peter's desperation, and (2) Jesus's reputation.

1. *Peter's desperation.* Peter has tried everything and has come up empty. Why not give Jesus a try? This is often true in our lives as well. We try everything we can in our own strength, and we only find failure. So Jesus is a last resort. The good news is that Jesus doesn't reject us just because we take a while to do it his way.

2. *Jesus's reputation.* Don't forget that Jesus has just healed Peter's mother-in-law in Peter's own house (Luke 4:38-39). Peter has witnessed Jesus's healing work firsthand. He's seen the crowds gather in awe of Jesus's miraculous actions. And he's just had a front-row seat to Jesus's amazing teaching preached from his own boat!

When these two things come together—feeling desperate after our failure to do it alone and witnessing or hearing about the power of Jesus—there's a good chance we'll turn to him, which is what Peter did. Peter takes a ho-hum tone: "OK, Lord, if you say so." Yet, despite his lack of enthusiasm, he receives an incredible, overflowing answer.

The nets are so full of fish that they are in danger of breaking! So the other boat comes over to help, and then even the boats are in danger of sinking!

Most of us have been like Peter at one time or another, saying unenthusiastically, "OK, Lord, if you say so."

To say Peter and his companions are astonished at the abundance of fish is an understatement. This is a catch like never before, a success beyond their wildest dreams. Later, those in the boat would witness Jesus calming a storm, and they would say, "Who is this? Even the wind and the waves obey him!" (Mark 4:41 NIV). In that moment, I can imagine them asking each other, "Who is this? Even the *fish* obey him!" This is like Christmas morning, a free cruise, and an unexpected windfall of money all rolled into one.

But once Peter calms down a bit, he realizes something. He begins to sense that this moment is about more than just fish—that Jesus is about to call him to do something more, to *be* something more. So he sinks to his knees in front of Jesus and begs him to leave.

Peter tells Jesus to "go away from me" not just because of his past but also because of what may come next. He's not the only one, of course, to resist a calling from God. Most persons in the Bible who are called by God begin by resisting their calling. Moses, Isaiah, Esther, and Jeremiah all tried to find loopholes to get out of their callings. Peter's insistence that he is sinful and inadequate to follow and serve follows a pattern of others in Scripture who have found the presence of God's holiness to be a spotlight on their own unholiness.

It's common for us to feel unworthy in the presence of the divine, but

God always answers with the assurance that it is not our worthiness that counts. God's power and holiness are what cleanse us when we're called to serve, and then he powers our ministry.

Also a common temptation is for us to see Jesus's miracles as an answer to our wish lists—just as it is a common anguish for us to wonder what we've done wrong if our dearest wishes haven't been fulfilled even after we have been faithful to God. As Peter witnesses this miracle of the abundant catch, he seems to be experiencing a dream come true and an undoing almost simultaneously.

Mark Buchanan imagines what is going through Peter's mind at this moment: the inner conflict between focusing on the abundance of wealth in the nets and focusing on the calling to follow Jesus. If Jesus's role is to fulfill our wishes, then he is there to serve Peter. But Jesus has something else in mind: for Peter to leave it all behind to serve Jesus. Buchanan writes:

> Jesus' calling is not to follow Peter. His role and task in life is not to advance Peter's career, enhance Peter's reputation, thicken Peter's wallet. Peter sees all that in Jesus's eyes. He sees that Jesus is not the man who exists simply to come onto our fish boats and fill up our nets. Peter must know what Jesus is about to say: "Follow me." Which means—ah, why does it have to mean this?—*leave everything*. The fish. The boat. The nets. The safety. The security. The prospects.
>
> *Leave everything.*
>
> Now imagine the moment. Peter falls on his face, begs Jesus to leave. *Depart from me.*
>
> Somebody's got to leave. Either Peter leaves everything, or Jesus leaves Peter.
>
> That happens every day somewhere. Jesus comes onto our boat and fills up our nets—a job promotion, a new house, a new car, a big raise. And our prayer is: "Oh, Lord, depart from me." Which means: Don't take it away. You leave me alone, Jesus, so

that I don't have to leave this behind. Go away and don't interfere
with my unbridled pleasure-taking in it.
But I'll call if the fishing gets scarce again.[6]

We have to remember what happens at the very end of this story. The
fishermen leave everything: the full nets, the boats, their careers, their families, and their homes. Everything they've ever had on a wish list is nothing
compared to following Jesus. When God brings abundance into our lives,
it's not the gift that deserves our attention, it's the Giver. All of the "abundance miracles" are simply indicators of the abundant God behind them
all—the One who desires our service, our worship, and our all.

Peter is a great example of abundance turning our hearts not to the gift
but to the Giver. When he first addresses Jesus in this story, he calls Jesus
"Master," the Greek name used to address tutors or teachers. But after he
pulls up the fish, he addresses him as "Lord."[7]

Have you professed that Jesus is Lord over everything you have and
everything you are today? Think about all the wishes and prayers you've
seen become reality in your life—all the abundance that is before you.
Now turn to the God in your boat—his eyes sparkling as he looks over the
nets and calls your gaze up from the catch to himself, saying: "Follow Me."

Are you in a place of emptiness? Has your *nothing* run out? If so,
that's good news because that's where Jesus's *everything* begins. When
we're hungry, Jesus feeds us not with anything of this world but with himself. He is our Bread of Life. He is the food we long for most. And he is
enough. Is there an impossible situation or need in your life, something
that makes you feel completely inadequate, insufficient, or helpless? Bring
your need to Jesus, offering him yourself and whatever resources you have.
Remember, he can do big things. He specializes in abundance. He's always
"able to do immeasurably more than all we ask or imagine" (Ephesians
3:20 NIV). He's not only enough—he is more than enough!

CHAPTER 3

MIRACLES ON THE WATER

EVEN THE WIND AND WAVES OBEY HIM

From an early age, I was fascinated with the Impressionist painters. Rembrandt is one of my favorites. While I've always admired the glorious colors and tranquil expressions of his portraits and still lifes, the one painting that captivates me most is full of both motion and emotion, *Christ in the Storm on the Sea of Galilee*. This is the only seascape that Rembrandt ever painted, and it's a tumultuous moment frozen in time. A small boat packed with disciples tilts precariously, almost capsized in the middle of a raging storm. Light and dark (Rembrandt's specialty) show us whitecap waves and dark clouds. The scene looks bleak, but if you look closely you can spot a hopeful patch of blue sky peeking through the storm, an indication of what's to come.

If you zoom in and search the anxious faces in the boat, you'll find them in all kinds of positions and postures: some are fighting the sails or straining at the oars, another is seemingly seasick over the side, one is praying, and some are turning toward Jesus. In the center of it all, a tranquil Jesus sleeps, resting just as peacefully as if safe on dry land. And when you do a head count, you'll find thirteen disciples in addition to Jesus at the center of the scene. Thirteen! If that number seems off to you, you're not alone.

The disciple smack in the middle of the painting is the only one seeming to make eye contact directly with us. His young face is distressed; he's hanging onto his hat even as he hangs onto a rope that keeps him from falling overboard. This young man's face at the center of the action looks remarkably like self-portraits that Rembrandt painted—and for good reason. Rembrandt painted himself into the center of his picture! It seems he got so personally invested in this biblical story that he literally put himself inside the scene he depicted on canvas.

God hears our cries over the rumble of the storm, and he knows our heart and our true need.

Of all Jesus's miracles, this is probably the one most of us can identify with. We've all experienced storms of chaos, anxiety, struggles, and worry. When life presents conditions that are chaotic and out of our control, we might take any of the postures found in the Rembrandt painting: bewildered, sick, fighting, praying, or reaching out to Jesus. Sometimes we even go through all of them! Finding out what happened in the moment of the real-life storm may give us some insight into how Jesus is present with us in the storms we're presented with on dry land.

Jesus in the Storm

Of all the miracles in the Gospels, the miracles on water are the only ones that Jesus performed just for the disciples. Of course, they were present for all of the miracles before this one as bystanders and sometimes beneficiaries. They got to eat some of the bread and fish and drink some of the wine. They watched in awe as people were healed, restored, and resurrected. But the venue for these particular miracles is much more private. The lake where Jesus first met many of the disciples becomes one of the last private places for him to address their needs, their fears, and their desperation. There are no crowds here. No wedding party. No bystanders along dusty streets. These miracles are personal because they address the disciples' desperate moments.

The region around Galilee was home for most of the disciples, and the lake at its center was known for its sudden and violent storms. Cool air masses from the surrounding mountains and fierce winds from the Golan Heights to the east often meet over the warm air of the lake, with resulting storms that crop up so suddenly they can catch even the most experienced sailors off guard.[1] Storms on the Sea of Galilee were common.

The storm must have been a doozy! The wind was high, the waves were rough, and the amount of water coming in was already threatening to swamp the boat. The reaction of the disciples said it all: they were terrified. Considering how many of them were professional fishermen, they would not have been disturbed by an insignificant squall. This was a major storm. The disciples honestly believed they were about to die!

While not all of us have been on a small boat in a life-threatening storm, we can all understand the fear and anxiety the disciples experienced. It's easy, like Rembrandt, to put ourselves "in the boat." We can also identify with the immediate and strong reaction of the disciples toward Jesus when their circumstances turned rough.

The disciples wondered if Jesus even cared. We can relate, can't we? When we are in the midst of extremely hard times, it's so easy to question whether God cares. These disciples had witnessed Jesus going out of his way to heal and help and save so many people from danger and distress. Now it seemed to them that he was sleeping through their hour of greatest need. The good news is that this was no surprise at all to Jesus. He knows our panic, our desperation, and our distress. God hears our cries over the rumble of the storm, and he knows our heart and our true need.

Jesus didn't waste any time responding to the disciples' concern. Jesus woke and jumped to action to take care of the immediate need of the disciples.

The story's placement is significant. It is right in the middle of a part of Mark's Gospel highlighting God's kingdom and rule and the truth that, because of God's reign, Jesus possesses the power needed to overcome evil and chaos. Mark 4 opens with Jesus telling story after story (parables) explaining God's kingdom and rule (vv. 1-34). Then Jesus uses that power to overcome the threatening chaos of the sea. And in chapter 5, when he reaches the other side, Jesus uses his power to do equally amazing things.

The storm in the middle of the lake is the centerpiece to God's actions of teaching about his power to the crowds on one side and enacting it for the crowds on the other. And here in the middle the disciples get a firsthand demonstration! God's power and compassion for his people are highlighted throughout this entire section.

Notice that Jesus does not enjoy or encourage storms in our lives. He is not seen in the story as the author of the storm but the One who puts it in its place. We see that Jesus "rebuked" the wind and the storm (4:39)—the same word given for his actions of rebuke against the evil spirit he encountered on the other side of the lake (5:1-20). And he spoke peace to the sea. The movement of the power of God is not toward chaos and fear but toward peace.

Just as Jesus's words had an immediate effect on the storm, they also had a powerful effect on the disciples. Notice that immediately after Jesus spoke to the storm he spoke to the disciples. He responded in love for these dear friends, who had just been shaking him and accusing him of indifference. Those words, "Be still," should have a familiar ring to them.

These words, "Be still," while they feel comforting, are actually a command. Being still in the presence of God, even when surrounded by difficult circumstances, is not something that comes easily to us. If it did, God would not have had to command us to do it. It's a discipline of obedience and trust, not just a natural gift some people have. When things are difficult, God commands us to be still and turn our eyes to him.

The disciples turned their eyes to Jesus and his power, and their attention and emotion changed from fear of the storm to awe of the Savior. The "great awe" described in Mark 4:41 could be translated literally: "They feared a great fear."[2] They began the scene in awe of the power the storm might have over their lives, and in the end they were in awe of the power Jesus had over the storm—and thus in their own lives as well.

We don't get to choose whether the sea we travel is calm or stormy, but we do get to choose where to turn our eyes and attention. We can choose to be overwhelmed by the power of the storms or overwhelmed by the power of God.

When we feel anxiety or fear at the chaos that every person encounters, we realize just how small and vulnerable we really are. There's a kind of fear that just perpetuates more fear, leading us into the circular thinking that more and more things could go wrong. But then there's a kind of fear that turns our attention to the awe of our Creator—the One who calms storms with words and walks upon the water.

Jesus Walks on Water

Some of the miracles in the Gospels make a lot of sense to me right off the bat. For example, why would Jesus heal a leper, a blind man, and a woman who was bleeding and outcast? Compassion or empathy, a sign of God's goal to move all of creation toward healing and wholeness. What does it reveal about God when Jesus feeds a crowd of hungry people? It is a picture of God's generosity, abundance, and the coming Kingdom where there will be no hunger or thirst. Why does Jesus raise people from the dead? Not only to heal and restore but also to show that he is Lord even over death, a foretaste of what will come in his own resurrection and ours as well.

But this one puzzled me at first: Why would Jesus walk on water?

What character trait does that display? Who does it help? Is anyone's life changed in this epic moment—a story so often told we don't usually bother to stop and ask why it happened?

Is this water walk a party trick? Is it "Hey, guys, watch this!"? That doesn't seem in character for Jesus. His actions are always purposeful, always reflect the character of God, and always move the kingdom of God closer to being a reality on earth as it is in heaven.

So, what is the message behind Jesus walking on water? I'd like to suggest three things.

1. Evil Is Real

Each of Jesus's miracles in some way combats the evil powers of the world and shows that God is triumphant over them. The natural world—with its brokenness of sickness, hunger, and death—is a world that Jesus acts to restore and remedy again and again. The spiritual realm—in which sins need forgiveness, relationships need restoration, and souls inhabited by evil spirits need deliverance—is also under God's power and rule.

So, how is evil vanquished by walking on water and calming storms?

In the first-century worldview, the sea symbolized the dwelling place of evil. The sea was unpredictable and tumultuous, often stirred with angry and life-threatening storms. Just as we often point upward when we think of heaven, in these ancient times the sea was seen as the home of "sinister power."[3]

The very beginning of Genesis shows the Spirit of God hovering over the waters. There is darkness, void, and emptiness, but God's Spirit is "over" them and prevails by creating order, light, and fullness.

By walking on water Jesus was treading on evil, crushing it under his feet.

This also is true in the story of Jesus calming the storm. When Jesus raised his voice to the evil realm that was threatening to sink the ship, silencing it with the words "Peace! Be still!" (Mark 4:39), he was showing that he has authority not only over the natural world but also over evil itself.

2. God, Who Triumphs Over Evil, Is with Us

While the disciples were ready for a hero, a new political leader, even a Messiah, they weren't always clear on the fact that Jesus was actually God in human flesh. Jesus would need to reveal that to them as they journeyed together over the years of ministry he spent with them.

Although Jesus's miracles pointed to the divine power working through him, that could have been explained as Jesus acting with a power that God gave him. The water miracles show Jesus's divinity, revealing that he was no messenger or middleman; he was God in person.

Though Jesus was fully God and fully human at all times, in some specific moments he aimed to help the disciples realize his identity as God in the flesh. So, when Jesus intended to "pass them by" (Mark 6:48), he was giving his disciples a clarifying moment of his true nature. God was showing himself to his people.

As the disciples witnessed a great storm calmed by Jesus's voice and saw him treading on the seat of evil, they began to realize that Jesus was no magician, powerful man, or even a miracle-working prophet; he was God in the flesh!

3. Do Not Be Afraid

As the disciples realized the immense gravity of the moment, learning that their rabbi, teacher, and friend was actually God, they were filled with all kinds of emotions. So Jesus immediately calmed them with these words: "Do not be afraid" (v. 50). This is also a common phrase in the theophanies of Scripture, always reassuring people of God's power.

When God reveals himself, people are filled with awe and fear. But God always reassures us that we don't need to be afraid—not of him or of anything that comes against us. God wants us to know that his immense power is matched by immense love, that he will work for our good, and that we can trust him.

Why did Jesus walk on water? Because evil is real; God, who triumphs over evil, is with us; and we need not be afraid.

We forget sometimes that the ordinary places are also where the extraordinary is most likely to happen.

Jesus was God in the flesh. Because of this, we can expect Jesus's character to reflect the character of God in Scripture. We can expect Jesus's actions to reflect the actions of God in Scripture. We can "take heart" and have no fear because God is with us!

Peter Walks on Water

In Matthew 14 we can see the awe and fear and even rising courage in Peter as Jesus calls him to take that step out of the boat. It finally registers with Peter that Jesus is walking on water, defying all kinds of natural laws. Peter must realize the power of God is at work in this moment, and he even dares to think that maybe that power might extend to him.

When Peter miraculously walks on water, the desperation is harder to see at first glance. But with a second glance, we'll swing our eyes around from Jesus on the water to the disciples in the boat and find Peter, poised on the edge. Interestingly, Matthew is the only Gospel writer who tells that Peter walked on the water too (vv. 28-33).

As in other stories of the disciples, Peter is once again at the center of the action. And, as in many other stories, we get to see Peter's impetuous nature, which often gets him into trouble, but in this instance gets him into the water to experience something no other disciple ever does.

As I thought about Peter's perspective, I couldn't help but wonder:

Where was his desperation? What was the "need" that drove him out of the boat, and what was the desperation Jesus was answering with his compassion and miracle-working power? To understand that, I had to search a little deeper into Peter's story.

Desperation in the Ordinary

The waters the disciples sailed on that night were waters where Peter had fished his entire life. The Sea of Galilee was one of those ordinary places for Peter. We all have them in our lives: places where we live day in and day out, going through the everyday, boring motions. Our house. Our commute. Our desk. Our kitchen. Their routines can hold predictable comfort or monotonous boredom. Peter spent many, many nights on the waters of Galilee having the same conversations and going through the same motions for the same small catch.

We forget sometimes that the ordinary places are also where the extraordinary is most likely to happen. I once saw a statistic warning that most car accidents occur within just a few miles of our own homes. *Of course*, I thought. *The streets closest to our homes are the ones we drive the most.* Likewise, the probability of getting "struck" by something life-changing is higher in those places where God finds us the most.

That fateful night when Peter and the disciples were out on the boat is one among thousands of nights Peter launched out into those same waters. The sea was Peter's backyard. His desk. His kitchen counter. But that night—in those familiar, ordinary surroundings—something extraordinary happened.

That night twelve disciples saw the same strange sight, felt the same terror, heard the same words, and experienced the same awe as Jesus walked effortlessly toward them when, by all natural understandings, he should have sunk. But, of the twelve, only one of them spoke up.

It would be wonderful to know exactly what was going through Peter's mind at that moment, but at least in part it must have been this: he wanted to be part of the amazing acts of God that he saw unfolding right before his eyes. To take a risk such as this, Peter must have been desperate to get out of that boat. But what was Peter desperate for? I'd like to suggest three things.

1. Desperate to Step Out of the Ordinary

Peter was asking for permission to step out onto the waters he knew all too well, the place he had spent many a monotonous night wondering if there was something more than the next wave, the next fish, the next day of doing it all over again. This was the site of Peter's commonplace life, the one he had left to follow Jesus, and he was begging for something more—to know the extraordinary in the ordinary place he knew well.

I don't know about you, but in my life God can sometimes become just another part of the routine. Church can be an appointment I put on my calendar—hours blocked off like any other time. Bible study or prayer time can sink into something repetitive to either check off or feel guilty that I did not check off. Then something happens to change all of that. Sometimes it's my own desperation—a sense that I long for more of the God I read about on the pages of the Bible to show up in a way that shakes up my self-focused existence. At other times it's hearing someone talk about God in a way that lights up his or her passion and eagerness for him. When people who have had a fresh encounter with God talk, it's as if he is as real to them as the person standing in front of them. When I hear that kind of enthusiasm for the Lord, it makes me hungry to know him on a deeper level. My prayers take on a new urgency, and my time seeking him gains new purpose. Suddenly I'm one of those people whose words inspire others to seek him. True love for God is indeed contagious.

2. Desperate to Conquer His Fears

Peter was asking permission to take a risk in a place where he had sought only safety. He had spent his life in awe and respect of these waters. Though he may have been familiar with the water and the boat, he also was familiar with the stories of fishermen who had not made it home from storms such as this one. One wrong step, one big storm, one leaky boat, and the sea would become his burial place. In this moment, Peter was asking permission to step out and tread upon the very thing that had struck fear in his heart his whole life.

Fears can take shapes of all kinds in our lives. Some are small, nagging thoughts that pop up from time to time. Others are raging terrors that fill us with anxiety. Sometimes our fears are connected to past hurts or incidents that caused us pain. The fear of repeating the past, whether it means falling back into old habits or becoming like someone who has hurt us, is a very real barrier to stepping out into the life God has called us to live. God doesn't want us to avoid our past and stuff down the fears and anxieties it may produce. He wants to bring us to such full healing that he can actually use our past experiences to minister to others through us. The places you've been hurt often will be the places you are most sensitive to see and hear the hurts of others. Don't let the fear of the past get in the way of what God wants to do in your future.

3. Desperate to Walk Toward Jesus

Notice that Peter's request was not to get out and run aimlessly around on the waves. Peter wasn't out for a thrill. He wasn't out to impress. He was headed in one direction: toward Jesus. He asked Jesus for an invitation, saying specifically, "Let me come to you." This wasn't thrill-seeking. It was Christ-seeking.

Peter wasn't just asking to defy the laws of nature. He was asking to defy the comfort that kept him imprisoned in his everyday routine. He was asking for the courage to defy the fears that had kept him in the boat. He was asking to be closer to Jesus. Expectations had sent him to the boat every day. Fear had kept him in the boat every day. Now he saw his Lord defy the expectations of both the comforts and fears of the world he had always known, and he said, "Lord, if it's real . . . if you're real . . . let me come to you."

Jesus simply said "Come," and Peter did (Matthew 14:29). He put one foot out of the boat and another in front of it, and he was walking on water toward Jesus! Don't miss the exciting meaning of this moment for you and me. If Jesus had just walked on the water by himself, it would have been enough to tell us that God is powerful beyond the ordinary. But because Peter also walked on the water toward Jesus, we know that God wants *us* to be participants in what he's doing in our world—that he wants to empower us to do far more than we could in our own power and strength.

When I think of miracles (and I've thought about them quite a bit lately!), I often pray that God will let me witness his work in very real and tangible ways. But here's the thing: God wants to be more than a curiosity that we witness from the sidelines. He wants us to jump in with him so that we can be his hands and feet right where the action is. Remember the servants back in Cana who were asked to fill the water jugs to the brim? It was their obedience that became participation in a miracle. They had the firsthand view that no one else had, simply because they were serving and obeying Jesus. When I ask God to show me his miracles, sometimes I feel his nudge to step into the places of greatest need and serve alongside him.

Worshipping a God who has the power to do the miraculous is one thing. It's another incredible step to realize that God wants us to share in this journey with him, to walk alongside him in ways we could never imagine without his help. On this journey of miracles, God doesn't leave us in the boat as casual observers. He calls us out into the excitement with him!

The Internal Battle

Peter is often criticized for what happened next. We're often quick to blame Peter for slipping into doubt and fear and beginning to sink, but who wouldn't have a moment of pause when they realize they are breaking the laws of nature? Who wouldn't doubt, being torn by the competing desires to join Jesus or to be safe? As a matter of fact, the Greek word for doubt, *distazo*, means "to attempt to go in two directions at once."[4]

To follow Jesus into scary, uncharted territory means each one of us goes through a kind of internal battle with the two directions we could follow at any moment: to look either at the Savior in front of us or at the waves beneath us.

Peter's story makes it clear that even the closest disciple in the middle of the most amazing display of God's strength will be torn between two desires: the desire to let Jesus call the shots and the desire to move back toward the safety and familiarity of controlling our own lives, even if it means a boring life of boat-dwelling.

"Lord, save me!" Peter cried, and then *immediately* Jesus reached out his hand (vv. 30-31). Thank God for that "immediately"! Without delay or hesitation Jesus responded by reaching where Peter was—doubt or no doubt—and saving him once again.

When we talk about being "saved" by Jesus, we are essentially saying this is our story too. We were sinking in something that was over our heads with our eyes focused on the peril and our fear, but we knew somewhere in the back of our minds that Jesus was right there, even if we weren't looking at him at first. Being saved by Jesus means seeing that the waves are too big for us but knowing that nothing is too big for him.

On another occasion when the disciples woke a sleeping Jesus and begged him to still the storm, they were asking him to take them from a place of danger to safety. But when Peter asked to get out of the boat, he was asking to move from a place of safety to danger. He was desperate to be desperate, and he got his wish. The waves were a place that challenged his fear to the utmost, and the same waves were a place that proved the willingness of his Savior to reach out and save him in a tight spot, even when the sinking was his own fault.

It was when he was sinking in the waves that Peter learned a lesson he would later need to draw upon again and again: that "Christ does not fail even those who fail him."[5]

God wants our attention fully on him, and he will stop at nothing to get it. But he also wants us to know that there is a life out there, greater than the ordinary, that we can be part of. Miracles of every kind, whether spectacular or more everyday, invite us out of the boat and into the journey with Jesus. Sometimes the invitation to journey with Jesus means bold prayer and courageous action, and sometimes the invitation is simply to be still in Jesus's presence.

Be Still

Stillness is not something most of us are good at. Our world today is one of continual motion. Many of us are in the business of busyness. Grownups are busy. Families are busy. Churches are busy. We run from one event and commitment to the next without much time to stop. Our bodies have been in motion for so long they sometimes forget how to be still. And, if we're not careful, it will make us sick.

Jesus lived out a pattern of action, rest, engagement, and reflection. In his humanity we find times where Jesus stopped and rested before or after important and tiring action in ministry. Today we read a story of Jesus staying behind to rest and take a break, even from his disciples. But we also find that the rhythm of rest is part of God's character and part of the Creation story.

God created us to live with a rhythm of rest. If you look at the story of Creation, as told in the first chapter of Genesis, you'll find a poetic story that captures this rhythm so well. For the first six days, the great masterpiece of Creation is described in an almost musical beat, with cadence and tempo, repeating words and phrases such as these:

> Evening and morning
> The first day, the second day, the third day, and so on
> And God saw that it was good . . . (and on the last
>   day God saw that everything was very good)

You could almost set a metronome to the reading of this first chapter of the Bible. There is such poetry here, such artistry in the telling. It's meant to mirror the artistry of the creation described. But it's only when you hear the rhythm of the first six days that you realize what happens so clearly on the seventh day, the last day of Creation, when that rhythm stops (2:1). On that day God finished. God rested. God blessed. That's it. No evening and morning, no good or very good. There's a very distinct feeling of putting on the brakes.

If the Lord of the universe could lay down his head and rest, it gives us great permission to stop and rest as well.

If Creation is the song of God's rhythms of creative work, then that seventh day called Sabbath is the rest in the score of music. If you play a piece of music and don't read the rests, you mess the whole thing up. But that's what we tend to do: we try to experience God's good creation without Sabbath rest.

Sabbath comes from the Hebrew word *sabbat*, which simply means "to cease," and the rhythm of stopping for one day of the week, just as God stopped—the rest at the end of the melody of the week—defined the song of the lives of God's people. Observing the Sabbath, or ceasing, was so important to God that it was listed in the Ten Commandments. "Remember the Sabbath day by keeping it holy. Six days you shall labor and do all your work, but the seventh day is a sabbath to the LORD your God. On it you shall not do any work, neither you, nor your son or daughter, nor your male or female servant, nor your animals, nor any foreigner residing in your towns" (Exodus 20:8-10 NIV).

We break this commandment far more often than any of the others. We are a people so in motion that it's hard to stop sometimes. It's a bit ironic that God, who can never be exhausted, chose to rest while we humans, who do get exhausted, often choose not to rest.

Ceasing activity to be with God on one day out of seven changes what happens *on* that day, but it also deeply affects what happens *in us* on the other six days. Giving our time to God in this way has the same effect as tithing a portion of our money: it reminds us that all we have is God's, and it sets our priorities for not just one portion of our assets but for all that we hold in stewardship for God.

God wants us to offer not just one day a week for him but all of our days. Creating rhythms of rest when we cease our work and frantic activity to stop and simply *be* doesn't have to wait for a single day. In fact, it shouldn't!

Jesus set the example for us. He certainly honored the Sabbath, but he also found other times to stop, ceasing motion and ministry, and connect in a deep way with his heavenly Father. Even as crowds pressed in, Jesus knew when he needed a break. We read, "Jesus began to teach by the lake. The crowd that gathered around him was so large that he got into a boat and sat in it out on the lake, while all the people were along the shore at the water's edge" (Mark 4:1 NIV). Note that Mark says Jesus got in a boat and sat in it out on the lake. He needed to get away from the crowd, to give himself a little space. Jesus had to physically remove himself from the craziness of the crowd to even be able to teach them, and he eventually found it was also a place he could get some time to rest.

The water miracles all happened around some of the busiest times of ministry for Jesus, and in these stories we even see him napping. Jesus knew how to live in the rhythm of rest and work, even if the crowds and the disciples didn't always understand what he was doing.

In Mark 4:35-38, when Jesus is finished teaching, he commands the disciples to leave the shore and sail across the lake, leaving the crowds behind. Here's where we encounter those words about Jesus's nap in the storm: "But he was in the stern, asleep on the cushion" (v. 38). Jesus was so tired, evidently, that he was able to sleep through a storm that frightened seasoned fishermen! I love that Jesus took naps. If the Lord of the universe could lay down his head and rest, it gives us great permission to stop and rest as well.

In Mark 6, we see that the crowds are again overwhelming, so Jesus calls the disciples away to a quiet place to get some rest. But the crowds follow them, and Jesus has such compassion on their needs that he teaches them many things and miraculously feeds them (vv. 30-44). We're told that after feeding the five thousand, Jesus sent his disciples ahead by boat.

I imagine that there was no end to the work Jesus could have done. He could have stayed with the crowds, continually meeting the never-ending needs of those brought to him. He could have stayed with the disciples, giving them much-needed instruction and answering questions until he had no more voice. Instead, he knew that he needed time alone with his heavenly Father.

Jesus knew not only that he needed rest from the demands of the crowd but also that the disciples would need time away as well. Repeatedly, he would direct them to retreat from the crowds for some time alone together. Jesus had a rhythm of rest and restoration that involved being actively and fully engaged with large groups of people, but that also required him to go away to quiet places to rest and be alone with his Father.

When we hesitate to stop and rest, it's as if we're saying that we are more important or our work is more needed than the work of Jesus. Friend, you and I are not the Messiah! We can lay our work aside and spend time receiving rest, prayer, and care from God just as Jesus did.

The Dance of Rest and Action

I grew up in Texas, and whenever someone said, "Let's go dancing," I always knew what they meant. They didn't mean ballroom or swing or salsa dancing. They meant the Texas two-step. The strange thing about the Texas two-step is that it's actually a dance that has *three* steps. I was taught to say under my breath with the steps, "Quick, quick, *slow*. Quick, quick, *slow*. Quick, quick *slow*." Though there are three steps, there are only two types of steps; thus it is called the two-step.

Now, here's the secret to two-stepping: you can't leave out a step. If you forget the slow step, things don't go well. You tend to trip over your partner and look foolish. Ask me how I know!

If you leave out the slow step, you really don't even have a dance anymore. Lots of quick steps with no slow step isn't a dance; it's a race. Imagine if you invited someone to dance and they started running. I'm sure that's not exactly the desired response to an invitation to dance.

God's command to rest is an invitation to dance—an invitation for you to return to his rhythm and observe the rests in the song of your life. Many passages in the Bible speak of this invitation to find rest in God's presence and how this affects our lives.

When we accept God's invitation to rest in his presence, we experience a divine reboot. We're reminded that we are finite creatures with limits and our worth is not in our work. We realize that our relationship with God is meant to be a dance, not a race.

Listen, we're all bad at this to start with. If we were great at it, God wouldn't have had to make it a command! If we knew how to do this instinctively, we wouldn't need the example of Jesus, who drew apart again and again.

We all get tired, burned out, and fatigued. But Jesus told us where to go with that fatigue. He calls us to come to him. And he promises that when we do, he will give us the gift of rest.

Because we see Jesus stopping periodically for rest, prayer, and reflection, we know that we must too. Sabbath is solid ground in a shifting sea of life. It's a way of giving one day to steady our nerves and remind ourselves again that we belong to God and are useful to him because of who we are, not what we do. Sabbath rest helps us recalibrate, reboot, retreat in a way that will remind us on every other day to come apart with God to enjoy him. It helps us find ourselves on steady ground again, and that is something we all desperately need.

The Miraculous Catch

Sometimes Sabbath rest means returning to that thing that you can't help but do. After an excruciating week, the disciples desperately needed to retreat and reflect, so what did they do? They went fishing.

The miracle of the gigantic catch seems like a sequel to an earlier encounter with Jesus. This miracle is the last one in the Gospels, performed even after Jesus's death and resurrection, but I'm including it here because it happened on the water. And like the other water miracles, its original audience was the disciples alone.

In this case, the disciples are approaching the end of the toughest week of their lives. They watched as their Savior and friend was arrested, tortured, and killed. And then, in a huge plot twist, he rose from the dead and appeared to them twice after that. You might say they are a little bit disoriented! Nothing has prepared them for the last few days of extreme lows and highs, moments of devastation and hope—and probably a lot of confusion.

When times are tough, many of us seek out something familiar. We go to a place that brings us comfort, or go talk to a person whose presence feels reassuring. I had a roommate that used to watch the movie *The Little Princess* every time she was sick or down. It comforted her to hear the familiar lines of her favorite movie. If we walked by her room and heard the lines from this movie playing, we knew she was in a bad place and trying to cheer herself up.

So, what did the disciples do when life seemed out of control? They went fishing!

I can see why the disciples might have headed to the water when they didn't know where else to go. Imagine if your Lord has been crucified and you are longing to hear his voice. Where do you go? If you want him to call you, instruct you, and work miracles on your behalf, you might just head back to the place where you first were called and instructed, the place you saw him perform miracles. You might go back to the boat.

61

We're told at the beginning of the story in John 21 that the disciples have been fishing all night and have caught nothing—which, if you've ever been fishing, you know is pretty typical. Waiting and catching nothing is probably the most common part of the fishing experience.

They are discouraged and are pulling their nets up when suddenly a figure calls out to them from the shore. When they obey and suddenly there are so many fish they can't even pull in the nets, a light bulb goes off. *This has happened before!*

The abundant catch that follows gets the fishermen's attention, to say the least, and Jesus captures their attention into an opportunity to call them to follow him as his disciples.

Now, as the resurrected Lord appears as a distant figure on the shore, the disciples once again know it is Jesus because of the abundance. Unlike the story from Luke, when they were relative strangers to Jesus and his remarkable gifts, here in John they have been with him throughout his ministry. They've seen him change water into abundant wine; they've witnessed the five loaves and two fish become an abundant meal for a crowd. And now this abundant catch has "Jesus" written all over it. This time they even count the catch!

Fishermen always measure and count. It's the only way to tell a good fish story! Clearly the abundance has captured their attention, but it's not what keeps their attention.

As we learned earlier, John's Gospel does not refer to miraculous events—healings, exorcisms, resurrections, acts of abundance—as miracles. No, John calls them signs. Signs have no value except to point to something else, and the miracles all point to Jesus.

The abundance isn't the point; the point is Jesus. The abundance, the signs, only exists to point us to him.

Most of the sequels I see these days (with two small children) are animated movies. One that my children adored was *Finding Dory*, the sequel to Walt Disney Pictures' *Finding Nemo*.

Finding Dory is about a fish (appropriate for a fishing story!) who is on a search for her family. She has short-term memory loss and has been separated from her parents, but she doesn't know how or where. The movie is about her search for them and the journey on which it takes her.

When Dory is little, her parents are aware of the danger of her getting lost and not being able to remember her way home. So they look for a tool that will get her attention and point her back to them. Dory loves shells, so her parents create trails of shells and teach her to notice them and follow them back to home, back to them.

In the most poignant scene of the movie, Dory, having been lost for years in the vast ocean, follows a trail of shells and finds at the end of it her loving parents, waiting there for her. It's a heartwarming reunion, but it gets even better. When the scene zooms out, we see multiple trails radiating out from their house like the rays of the sun. Every trail points back to home, back to the place where those who love Dory best are waiting for her. Her parents had prepared in abundance for the purpose of leading her home.

In a similar way, God uses the abundance in our lives to get our attention and then turn it to him. If we keep our eyes on the abundant things, we are missing the point. They are not signs that point to themselves but abundant trails that lead us home to God.

Most of the time, abundance gets our attention. If Jesus is associated with abundance, I'm sure there is some kind of abundance we'd all like to ask for. "Yes, Lord," we say, "I'd like an abundance of _____." Funds. Chocolate. Compliments. Vacations. Well-mannered children. Job offers. You fill in the blank.

But sometimes the trails leading us to seek Jesus are a different kind of abundance—abundance of need, abundance of worry, or abundance of realization that we just aren't making it on our own. While God may not be the author of adversity, he certainly won't waste a sign if he can turn it to point you to him. All of these things can point you to the One who has been searching for you all along, lining up signs to direct you to him.

You may remember that Peter's response in the first abundant catch story was different from his response the second time. The first time, the miraculous presence of a holy God caused Peter to notice his own sin. But later, after all Jesus and Peter had been through together, Peter actually dropped everything, including the catch! He swam away from the huge catch of fish and toward the Lord. Peter was more aware of his own sin than ever before because the last time he saw Jesus alive, he denied him. But as much as Peter knew his own sin, he knew even more the abundance of grace and forgiveness that is in Jesus. That abundance inspired Peter not to wait for the boat to row ashore but to swim to Jesus.

Whether you're facing an abundance of reasons to believe in God's power or an abundance of desire to look for those reasons, follow that trail. Let the good and the bad point you to Jesus.

The psalmist says, "Surely goodness and mercy shall follow me / all the days of my life" (Psalm 23:6). The Hebrew word for *follow* in this passage literally means "chase." Goodness and mercy are chasing after you, hunting you down, trying to find you. The irony for those of us who think we have been searching for God is that he has been chasing us all along!

Maybe you're in a stormy life, needing comfort. Or maybe you're in a comfortable place needing a life. Jesus is there. He's not a God far away with no understanding of pain or distress or grief. He's God in the boat, God treading out on a dangerous place over a sea of evil to get to us. God on a cross.

I hope you sense God calling you to him deeper than ever before, calling you to cling to him in the storms you're going through, or calling you out of the boat to deeper waters, riskier and more wonderful than you'd ever imagine. His call is the same for you today as it was for the disciples: *Follow me.* Whether that means leaving your nets, clinging to him through storms, or stepping out in faith, know that he's there. He's in the same boat. And you can trust him with your life!

CHAPTER 4

JESUS OUR HEALER

OUR BROKEN PLACES IN HIS HEALING HANDS

G od's work is slow, even imperceptible sometimes. This is often the case in our lives, and Jesus often has to repeat his process more than once in order for someone's healing to be complete. Or, as they might say in Texas, some nails need more than one hit.

One of God's characteristics as Creator that I've always been most grateful for is that he stays interested in and engaged with his creation. Although God could have cried "Done!" on the seventh day of Creation and walked away—or could have easily given up on us during our multiple mess-ups throughout human history—the fact is that he never leaves us or gives up on us. In my own life, I've reached points of discouragement so deep that I was sure things were broken beyond repair, but the reminder that my Creator is still waiting to heal, restore, and remedy the injustice and brokenness around me has kept me from giving up many times. No matter how broken people or situations may seem, nothing is beyond God's healing hand.

As we see in the Gospels, most of the miracles Jesus performed were healings. One-fifth of the Gospels—or 727 of the 3,779 verses—concern healing of some kind. That's a remarkable amount of emphasis on healing.[1]

Why did Jesus spend so much time healing people and talking about healing? One obvious reason is that he had compassion on people who were sick—people whose lives were broken and whose hearts were desperate. He had the power to change their lives, and so he did. But there's an even bigger picture of God's heart here that reveals to us how he wants us, his children, to live: restored and whole.

If we look at the bigger picture of God's purposes for the world as communicated in Scripture, we see that his hopes for us do not include sickness or death. The story of Creation, painted in the first two chapters of Genesis, shows a harmonious existence with no sickness or death or brokenness of any kind. Even the relationship between God and his people and their relationships with each other are unblemished by any kind of shame or division.

If we want to understand God's heart for healing, we need to remember that he does not desire pain, sickness, or death for his people. Those things entered the world through human sin and evil, and all of Scripture, from the first chapter of Genesis through the last chapter of Revelation shows God's work of stamping out these things and reconciling his people to himself.

Since Jesus was God walking in flesh on the earth, we can see the ultimate purposes of God through Jesus's actions, words, and relationships. This means that if we want to know what the heart of God looks like, we can see it in the life and ministry of Jesus. So, if someone ever tells you that sickness or pain or death came from God, just look at Jesus's life and you'll see that he never used his miraculous power to cause anyone sickness or pain or death. Actually, whenever he encountered these things, he set about to reverse them. Each personal healing Jesus performed is a small picture of God's grand plan for his creation. Let's explore a few of these stories and what they have to teach us.

The Man with Leprosy (Matthew 8; Mark 1; Luke 5)

In Matthew 8:1-4; Mark 1:40-45; and Luke 5:12-16, we encounter a man with a terrible skin disease. When we hear that this man was *covered* with leprosy, we might think about how much he must have suffered. But in some ways, it didn't matter how mild or severe his condition was. In those days, even a tiny spot of leprosy changed the course of a person's life forever.

Those with leprosy were forced to live together just outside the city gate and were required to shout "Unclean!" if anyone approached them to protect the other person from coming too close. Lepers also had to change their physical appearance to show that they were outcasts, so that no stranger could miss the fact that they were unclean. Because lepers were considered spiritually unclean, touching someone with leprosy would make that person spiritually unclean as well, and that would require him or her to go for a checkup and spiritual cleansing by a priest. A person's entire world—physical, social, spiritual, and cultural—would be turned upside down by the diagnosis of leprosy.

With this understanding of the requirements for persons with leprosy, it is shocking that this man did not keep the prescribed distance but approached Jesus. He must have heard about or witnessed Jesus's healing power, so he chose to take a huge risk.

In each of the Gospel accounts, the man came close to Jesus and lowered himself. Luke recounts that he lowered himself so much that he put his face on the ground and begged, throwing himself at Jesus's feet.

Don't miss this powerful combination of boldness and humility! Because of his diagnosis and social shame, the man was supposed to stay at a distance from others. According to popular understanding, he was unclean, unworthy, and undeserving of Jesus's attention. But in his desperation, he became bold and willing to ask for Jesus's help. Yet when he approached Jesus boldly, his posture wasn't one of arrogance or entitlement but humility—*begging.* The combination of these two postures of boldness and humility was powerful then, and it is powerful now. We need the boldness to go to Jesus in our desperation and the humility to know we need his mercy when we get there.

This combination of the boldness to approach Jesus and the humility to bow before him is the posture of prayer. It's the posture of abandonment in the presence of the Holy. It's a posture of the heart, not just of the knees. And it's a posture that pleases God. God loves our willingness to come to him and ask for what we need in the same way that a caring parent loves to hear a humble and genuine need from their child.

So the man at Jesus's feet cried out in bold humility: "Lord, if you are willing, you can make me clean" (Luke 5:12 NIV).

Now hold your breath as you read what happened next because it's shocking: "Jesus reached out his hand and touched the man" (v. 13 NIV).

Jesus *touched* this man—this contaminated man who was thought to be unclean and would defile anyone he touched, this lonely man who possibly had not been touched by anyone in years. There are healings of leprosy in the Old Testament, such as in Numbers 12 and 2 Kings 5, but even in those situations, Moses and Elisha didn't dare touch the persons being healed. Touch means connection, relationship, and acknowledgment—and these are hallmarks of Jesus's healing ministry. Don't miss the fact that Jesus reached out and touched this man *while he was still covered in leprosy*—while he was unclean with a disease that everyone would now say Jesus was unclean with as well.

The understanding of leprosy was that it was too contagious to risk touching or even being near the infected person. But Jesus's cleanness was more contagious than the man's uncleanness. And this is good news for us, too! Jesus's holiness is always more powerful than the problems he encounters in our lives. There is nothing in us—or in anyone else—that is so damaged Christ will not lovingly touch when we ask with bold humility.

The passage tells us that *immediately* the leprosy left the man and he was healed. Then, Jesus sent him to the priest, in effect reconnecting the man with his community. Jesus had healed his disease, but now the man needed to be declared clean to be restored in relationship to those he loved. Here's another amazing truth: Jesus's goal for us is always more than a physical cure; it's restoration in community with others and with God himself.

At the end of the story, Jesus calls on the man to give testimony to those in his community of what had happened. Jesus knows that when we tell others how our lives have been touched by God, it makes the cleanness even more contagious because their lives are touched as well.

God wants *us* to approach him with bold humility and offer him our needs. He wants us to know that there's nothing so damaged in our lives that it would deter him from touching us. *Nothing.* We need to know this not only for ourselves but also for the sake of others, because sometimes we are called to carry others in need of healing to Jesus.

Carried to Jesus (Mark 2:1-12)

Our young adult small group had been meeting in my living room every Thursday night for a few months. There were singles and couples, parents and nonparents. This group of fun-loving, smart, engaging believers in Jesus was digging deeper each week both into God's Word and into relationship with one another. Each week the questions grew deeper and more personal, and the conversation and fun got louder.

At the end of our time together each week we would ask for prayer requests. Unlike the rest of our time together, the prayer request time seemed to be the quietest point of our gatherings. We were in that stage of community where we were hesitantly learning just how vulnerable we wanted to be with our own deepest concerns and needs. One young married couple spoke up hesitantly, asking us to pray for an "unspoken" prayer request.

We knew what the word *unspoken* meant: they needed prayer but weren't comfortable sharing what it was about. The next week they lifted up the same request. This went on for several weeks, but they didn't elaborate. And, honestly, no one in the group had the courage to ask for more information. Then one week they didn't show up. The next week they were absent as well. I called the wife to ask if everything was OK. She hesitated for a moment, took a deep breath, and then said, "We're getting a divorce. We've tried everything, and it's just never going to work. We won't be coming back to the group."

I could hear the pain and struggle in her voice as we talked. As I listened to my friend and asked questions about what they had been through, she admitted that this was the first they had told anyone. They hadn't spoken out loud of the situation to their family or friends or our group. They hadn't been to our pastor for help or sought marriage counseling. I began to wonder what she meant by "we've tried everything" when they hadn't tried the support of the community around them. The more isolated they had become in their secret struggle, the worse it had become. My heart broke for them.

One of the hardest things in life is to admit that we need help. None of us likes to confess to others that we don't have it all together or that we don't know how to handle a problem. And yet most of us would be willing, even eager, to help if someone came to us with the same need. We are much more comfortable being the ones who help others than needing help ourselves.

In Mark 2, we encounter the remarkable love of a group of friends. There's so much we don't know about them. We don't know how long they had known each other. We don't know how long the man on the mat had been paralyzed or what caused his problem. We don't even know if the man they carried came willingly or if his friends insisted despite his doubts or objections. What we do know is that they cared about their friend and wanted to see him get well. We know they believed in Jesus's power enough to carry their friend to Jesus.

In community, sometimes we are those who carry, and sometimes we are those who are carried.

Being the friends who carried this man to Jesus was a task of hard, heavy work. They had to find the right materials and route, communicate and balance with each other, and keep a pace all four could agree on and manage. If you've ever carried furniture with other people, imagine balancing a physically fragile person on the top of that furniture! But the men cared enough about their friend to be inventive and resourceful. They were determined to get him help. They were so determined that when they arrived at the house Jesus was teaching in and found that the crowds extended outside the doors, they still looked for a way to get their friend in front of this healer. They loved him too much to give up.

Unlike our shingled roofs, Capernaum homes, covered with beams that had branches and reeds over them, held together by dried mud, would have been much easier to dig through. Even so, imagine this group digging a hole big enough to lower a man through—and then coordinating their effort to lower him to the floor without dropping him! Their task wasn't easy, and it ended with a mess in someone's living room. But their love for their friend was greater than the obstacles in their path.

Imagine what it was like to be the friend who was carried to Jesus. What would it be like to be unable to care for yourself? How would you react to friends who wanted to go to all lengths for you? What would you say when they hatched a crazy plan and began carrying you through the streets, making a spectacle that ended with climbing onto a house, digging through a roof, and lowering you to the floor inside? I can imagine myself saying things like, "Please, don't go to all this trouble just for me" or, "Hey, you almost dropped me!" The man's emotions may have ranged from feeling insecure to annoyed to unworthy of such bold actions.

Being the person who needs help is not easy. Most of us would rather carry the mat than be carried. But we all need carrying sometimes. The Bible paints a picture of community where our burdens are not our own.

They are to be shared with others when needed but never in a way that is unhealthy or exempts us from personal responsibility.

Throughout the Scriptures we are reminded to carry each other's burdens. The Greek word for "burden" in Galatians 6:2 is *baros*, which means a weight or a heavy load, a boulder that is too heavy to carry alone.[2] If someone has a boulder to bear, he or she needs help from their community. Then in verse 5 we're reminded that each should carry his or her own load. The word for load in Greek is *phortion*, which refers to an individual pack that one person would carry.[3] Think of this as a backpack. So we are meant to carry a backpack load by ourselves, not a boulder load.

Overload isn't good for any of us, and when we see someone struggling, we often are able to use the strength God has given us to come alongside the person and help. But we need to remember not to become enablers who pick up so many backpacks of others, which they could carry on their own, that the weight becomes a burden on us. In order to decide when to help and when to step back, we often have to pray and seek God's guidance as well as ask others for advice.

Once the man was lowered to the ground of a now messy house with a disassembled roof, Jesus surprised everyone by declaring, "Son, your sins are forgiven" (Mark 2:5). Remember, Jesus wants to heal the whole person—spiritual, physical, emotional, relational—so he started with the man's sins. The reaction around him was anything but positive.

The religious experts in attendance knew that only God could offer forgiveness and that, in their religious system, forgiveness was given through sacrifices made by the high priest at the temple. Jesus's statement seemed blasphemous to them, as if he were claiming to be God.

But Jesus wasn't done. He continued, healing the man's body as well as his soul. As evidence of this, Jesus commanded the man to get up, pick up his mat, and walk. The man who had been carried in was now carrying his own burden out!

We're told that everyone was amazed and praised God. *Everyone.* That means that the doubting and outraged Pharisees were also praising God in amazement! This miracle of healing pointed people to the truth about Jesus: he *is* the Son of God, able to heal bodies and forgive sins.

The group of friends had been right to bring their struggling friend here. They knew better than to believe they could fix their friend's problems themselves, but they knew that Jesus was the One who could.

At times our burdens will outweigh our ability to carry them. We'll find ourselves desperate and needing to depend on others, or we will sink beneath the load. God paints a picture of community as a place of shared struggle and shared joy. This is the role of Christian community: We share strength when we have it; we ask for help when we need it. Sometimes we're on the mat; sometimes we carry it. But it's always right to bring our own needs, and those of our friends, to Jesus. He is the answer to every burden. And he alone has the power to heal.

Jesus Speaks and Evil Flees
(Matthew 17; Mark 9; Luke 9)

In our modern culture we almost never use words such as *demons, possession*, and *exorcism*. Just typing those words on a laptop in the twenty-first century seems so strange. For some, those ideas may seem archaic in the age of science; for others, evil and the spiritual topics associated with it are much more a part of their vocabulary. Depending on the church traditions in which we've grown up (if any at all), the idea of Jesus freeing a little boy from demon possession can be challenging to understand and apply to our lives. Yet in this healing story, we find Jesus performing a miracle that can help us understand more about our God who heals.

Jesus shows us God's desire to come to the rescue of his children—oftentimes with just a word.

Healing is a big part of what Jesus was about in his ministry of restoring God's kingdom on earth, and releasing people from demons was one of the types of healing miracles that Jesus practiced. Today when we think of healing, we often focus on the symptoms of our physical bodies. But in Jesus's culture there was no dividing line between a person's physical, spiritual, and emotional well-being. In many ways we are rediscovering this today, as doctors and researchers are finding evidence that much of our emotional and physical health are bound up together.

Biblical passages about demon possession have sometimes been read by the church in ways that have been harmful to people who are suffering from diseases such as epilepsy or mental illness. We should never assume that symptoms we can't understand or see a root cause for are necessarily rooted in spiritual causes. Jumping to conclusions that human symptoms have demonic roots can be damaging to the persons affected. On the other hand, just because we cannot see, control, or even fully understand something does not mean that it's not real. The Bible often helps open our eyes to the unseen spiritual roots of visible realities.

In the culture in which Jesus lived and performed miracles, it was very common to speak about demons and be released from the power of demons through exorcism. Some interpret these texts as metaphors, talking about how we can be "freed from our demons," or our struggles. And there is certainly truth in the idea that our own struggles are sometimes our demons. But others believe that it's clear Jesus was talking in these passages about, and even talking *to*, something or someone. We're often much more comfortable talking about the spiritual beings embodied in the good (angels) than we are wondering if there are opposite forces at work for evil.

It was actually so commonplace in Jesus's day for people to talk about and witness the personification of evil in demons or "impure spirits" that their reactions to Jesus's miracles may seem a little ho-hum to us. In the first chapter of Mark's Gospel, Jesus frees a man from an unclean spirit, and it is a pretty confrontational and chaotic moment. Jesus shouts, "Be quiet!

... Come out of him!" and then we read, "The impure spirit shook the man violently and came out of him with a shriek" (Mark 1:25-26 NIV).

Now, if this happened in the middle of a crowd today, people would be aghast. And the people watching Jesus were too—but not for the reason we might expect.

Think about the significance of this healing. The amazement the crowd expressed at Jesus's command over the spirit was secondary to the fact that Jesus had simply used words or commands to produce results—nothing more. This emphasized to the people Jesus's incredible power and authority over evil. His power can be displayed simply by speaking a word, as we've seen in other miracle stories.

Again and again in the Gospels, Jesus shows us God's desire to come to the rescue of his children—oftentimes with just a word.

The emphasis in this story of the demon-possessed boy is on *faith*. First, the boy's father complained to Jesus that the disciples had already tried to help his son and had failed. Jesus's response was to chastise the disciples for their lack of faith: "You unbelieving generation," and then he told the father, "Bring the boy to me" (Mark 9:19 NIV). The disciples had been trying to do this on their own, without relying on Jesus. And Jesus reminded them that he alone is the source of healing.

The way to help others is not in our own strength but to bring them to Jesus, something we can do through prayer.

The next part of the story that highlights faith is the moment when we clearly see how desperate the father was. Nothing brings parents to their knees like their desperate love for their children. It is both the most wonderful and most vulnerable kind of love there is.

Jesus responded to the father's request by saying, "Everything is possible for one who believes" (Mark 9:23 NIV), and the father responded in verse 24 with what is, for me, one of the most cherished phrases in all of Scripture: "I do believe; help me overcome my unbelief!"

The father expressed a desire to believe wholeheartedly in Jesus while at the same time he confessed a cautious, tentative hope. He had faith, but he lacked faith. If we're honest, most of us in our greatest moments of need could say the same thing to God. We are a people who have faith and need faith all at once.

We can easily slip into the fear that without *perfect* faith, our cries for God's help will be ignored. But praise God, Jesus's response of healing this little boy shows us that this isn't the case! This story tells us that Jesus's powerful response to our needs isn't a result of our own piety or certainty; it is because of the grace of God himself.

At the end of this miracle story, the disciples asked Jesus where they went wrong. Jesus's answer was plain and simple: prayer (vv. 28-29).

In other words, prayer is the power source for God's miraculous work in our lives. When we feel a lack of power or faith, we can lean into our source of power found through our communion with God in prayer. Evil is real; that's certain to anyone who's paying attention in life. But Jesus is more powerful than evil. More powerful than sickness. More powerful than death. He has the power to heal us—physically, spiritually, and emotionally—and he has ultimate victory over all evil. That's something we can be certain of!

Of course, it has to be said that our prayers for healing may not always result in the answers we ask for or on the time schedule we hope for. We are certain of God's power and victory; we can also be certain of God's goodness and mercy. When God's timing doesn't match our plans, it can be confusing for us and especially for those who might be skeptical of God's ability or willingness to answer prayers in the first place. Thankfully, God can handle our prayers, our faith, and even our doubt.

The Syrophoenician Woman (Mark 7)

When I spotted the event announcement in a magazine highlighting classes for local writers, it was as if they had created an event just for me:

All-Night Write-In—8:00 p.m. to 8:00 a.m.
Join a group of local writers overnight for writing sprints,
fellowship, and guaranteed progress on your current project. Pizza,
snacks, and breakfast provided.

As a lifelong night owl and pizza lover, I knew I had to attend! At three in the morning, though, bleary-eyed and jittery from too much coffee, I was wondering if it had been such a great idea. My progress had started off at 8:00 p.m. with a rushing river of ideas, and it had slowed to a babbling brook around 11:00 p.m. Now here it was 3:00 a.m., and there was not even a trickle.

During a break, a similarly groggy group began gathering near the coffee, waiting for a fresh pot to brew. As we got to know one another, people began sharing what they were writing. An older woman was writing mysteries, while her friend who came with her was writing poetry. A seventeen-year-old girl kept glancing at her phone: she had convinced her parents to let her stay past her curfew, promising that she would finish college essays although she really wanted to write short stories. A twenty-something man in an orange T-shirt and saggy jeans said he was working on a dystopian novel. Then, suddenly, they were all looking at me.

"Miracles," I blurted out. "I'm writing a book about miracles and how our desperation is actually a good thing because it's what comes before a miracle."

Since writers are a pretty unusual crew anyway, they didn't bat an eye at the odd subject matter. But one of the older women spoke up, saying matter-of-factly, "Except they don't happen to us. You can pray for a miracle all you want, but no one is really listening." I wondered for the rest of the night about that woman, wishing I knew her story and what unwritten miracle she had been waiting for that hadn't happened.

One of the most difficult issues to address when talking about miracles, especially healing miracles, is the question of unanswered prayer.

Many of us have prayed—or are currently praying—for healings that haven't happened. It can cause us to doubt God, to doubt ourselves, to become angry or jealous, and to feel forgotten.

But we discover through the Scriptures that our lives and the cries of our hearts matter to God. He tells us that he knows us *intimately*.

God knows the number of hairs on our heads, and although he pays attention to the tiniest of birds, we are worth more than a whole flock of them! When you wonder if God sees you, hears you, and cares about you and your concerns, remember that it's just not possible for God to forget about you.

While the details of our hearts' most intimate cries are important to God, our perspective on his eternal story must always be bigger than the rise or fall of one set of circumstances. I want to encourage you to keep three things in mind when prayers go unanswered.

1. Don't Assume You Are a Second-Class Citizen

Sometimes when prayers go unanswered, we may feel like second-class citizens in the kingdom of God, as if God has heard and cared about the concerns of others but forgotten about us. I know, when my own prayers have lingered in the unanswered column, I've wondered if God was really listening or if there was some reason he was withholding the blessings I considered so easy to bestow.

All of those God has made are good in his eyes. God has no second-class citizens!

If anyone could have felt like a second-class citizen in Jesus's presence, it would have been the Syrophoenician woman in Mark 7. It's unfortunate that we don't know her name, but we're reminded of a central point about her every time we call her "the Syrophoenician woman." Mark tells us in his Gospel, "The woman was a Gentile, of Syrophoenician origin" (7:26).

This description tells us that she was not Jewish, which meant that she was an outsider to the Jewish faith. Being Jew or Greek was a dividing line among the people in that culture, and Jews often looked down on people outside the faith as those undeserving of God's blessings. A common misconception among the Jews was that their status as God's chosen people meant that God would bless them but not others.

The Jews in Jesus's day did not expect much faith from pagan outsiders, especially from a pagan woman such as this one.[4] And they would have remembered that the most prominent woman from Phoenicia, which was the same region where the Syrophoenician woman was from, was the wicked Jezebel. So it must have been surprising when this woman dared to come inside a house where Jesus was staying and approach him boldly, falling at his feet and asking him to heal her daughter from demon possession. Those gathered around might have been shocked that she would dare come to Jesus at all—and perhaps even more shocked by his response.

Before we get to Jesus's response, let's take a step back and look at the full chapter of Mark 7 where this story is found in order to find a clue about why Jesus responded to her as he did. In the previous verses in this chapter, Jesus had a conversation with the Pharisees about things that would make a person spiritually clean—able to come into worship and into contact with God with a pure heart—or unclean. While the Pharisees were arguing that the most important thing in maintaining purity before God was washing hands in a certain way before eating or avoiding certain foods because they were clean or unclean, Jesus had other ideas.

Jesus went on to shock the crowd he had called around him by telling them there were no longer any unclean foods for Jews since what is in people's hearts is the true indicator of righteousness, not what is in their stomachs (vv. 14-23). Shortly after his conversation with the Pharisees, Jesus encountered the woman from Syrophoenicia (vv. 24-30). And after his conversation with her, as he was traveling through a region called Sidon, Jesus healed a non-Jewish man who was deaf and mute (vv. 31-37). These stories are a three-part package in which Jesus loudly proclaims that God's creation—the food he has made and especially the people he has made—are good in God's eyes.

So, with this insight, let's return to the unusual exchange between Jesus and the woman when she asked him for healing for her daughter.

In verse 27, Jesus sounds like he is telling a riddle. "Let the children be fed first, for it is not fair to take the children's food and throw it to the dogs." This comment has puzzled many and made them wonder if Jesus was dishonoring the woman by referring to her in this way. Yet we need to remember that Jesus was referring to the Jews as "children" in the same way that Exodus 4:22 says, "Israel is my firstborn son."

Jesus was reiterating the idea of Israel being the firstborn in the family of God; however, that relationship was for the sake of saving the *whole world*. All of those God has made are good in his eyes. God has no second-class citizens!

Remember that no matter if your prayers fall into the answered or unanswered column, you are precious to God! He made you, he loves you, and he is always listening and longing for relationship with you.

2. Don't Stop Praying

When our prayers go unanswered, we can be tempted to quit praying. *After all, what's the point?* we may wonder. But we can learn a lesson in persistence from the Syrophoenician woman.

Rather than give up and walk away, she rebuts the riddle, "Lord . . . even the dogs under the table eat the children's crumbs" (Mark 7:28). She's saying that even the lowliest member of the family deserves to be fed. This comment is evidence of her determination and persistence before God. Her request for a small crumb of Jesus's mercy indicates that she believed even the smallest fraction of his power would heal her daughter. This was a big vision of God for a woman who had been shut out of the community of faith. And we know from other miracles what Jesus can do with the smallest of crumbs!

Once, after a significant move of God in my life resulted in some big changes for my family, a friend I hadn't talked to in a few years called. She had heard about my good news from a mutual friend and had called to rejoice with me. Then she reminded me of a prayer group we had been in together ten years earlier. She remembered that I had asked for prayer around this same issue and that our group had lifted me up in prayer. "Jessica," she said, "those are ten-year-old prayers we just saw answered." I was amazed, both at her incredible memory and at the fact that God hadn't forgotten our petitions!

If answers to your prayers seem far off, don't back away from God. Lean in. Keep praying with bold humility. In Scripture, blessings often come to those who will not give up in their pursuit of God.

According to the Gospel of Mark, Jesus won every controversial conversation he had with the religious authorities, yet he allowed himself to be persuaded by this desperate parent. Take that in for a moment. Desperate persistence moves the heart of God! This story encourages us to keep asking, knocking, and persisting in prayer when it seems that our petitions are not being answered. Though we may not get the outcome we've asked for in prayer, we can always count on being blessed in response to our persistent faith.

3. Don't Forget that God's View Is Bigger than Ours

A third thing that can happen when prayers go unanswered is that we can develop tunnel vision. We can become so focused on our unmet requests that we fail to see the bigger picture of all God is doing in and around us. As we persist and seek God in prayer, we must keep in mind that our human view is so much smaller and more limited than God's all-encompassing and eternal view.

Imagine the prayers the disciples prayed on Good Friday as Jesus was beaten, condemned, and then executed on the cross. Don't you imagine that every single one of the disciples prayed for things to go differently?

And was anyone ever as deserving of those prayers being answered as Jesus was? In the disciples' short view of the situation, their prayers went unanswered. But then came Easter! God had a longer view, a plan that would change their lives and the entire world forever.

A friend who struggled for years with infertility recently told me the story of the desperate prayers she prayed before God for a child of her own. She told me that for years her prayer was, "God, if you give me a baby, I will love you and serve you forever." Years passed as she prayed that prayer when one day she realized that her heart had changed. She was now praying, "God, even if I never hold my own child in my arms, I will love you and serve you forever."

If we pray long enough, it's highly likely that we all will have prayers that remain unanswered. But even the act of persistent prayer leads us to the source of comfort, mercy, and truth. Our prayers may not always elicit the exact response we're longing for, but they always end in a connection with Christ. When we make the effort to pray, we know that God hears and that our prayers, even when they're full of frustration and anger, are beautiful in God's ears. Jesus's compassionate response to a persistent woman who was an outsider shows us that he is listening and hears our cries. My friend whose prayers seemed to be met with silence for years was telling me the story of her seemingly unanswered prayers as she held her new baby, a miracle and an answered prayer. She was remarking at what a changed heart she had, not because her wishes had been realized but because she knew now that her love for God wasn't based on the condition of getting what she wanted from him. Her changed heart happened before her prayers were answered.

We can know with confidence that we are loved and heard by God! Unanswered prayer and unreceived blessings are some of the hardest hurdles that those of us who follow Jesus deal with. But the best place for us to be when we are hurting or uncertain or even angry is in God's presence. Whether or not your prayers lead to the answer your heart longs for, they lead you to Jesus, which is what his heart longs for! Don't give up praying, and know that God will never give up listening. God's heart is kind, and his name is Love. God is inclined to move with compassion as we see over and over throughout Scripture.

The Man by the Healing Pool (John 5)

The man in this story from the Gospel of John had been sick his entire life. His sickness had a lifespan longer than many people even lived in the first century—thirty-eight years. He was alone, with no family to assist or comfort him. He spent his days gathered with other sick people around a pool they thought was their only hope for healing. Their lives were defined by illness: the blind, lame, and crippled, all hoping for healing. They weren't well enough to work or pure enough to go to the temple, so their illness created its own kind of community for them. The pools themselves were the reason they gathered there: a superstition held that whoever got in the pool first when the waters were stirred or bubbling would be healed. But with such a backlog of the sick, it's unlikely their desires for magical healing were placed in something worthy of that kind of hope.

When Jesus stood over the man, perhaps blocking his view of the pool that held his hopes for healing and the community that held his identity in sickness, it was a moment that was completely unexpected. The man hadn't seen Jesus or called him over, but for some reason Jesus singled him out among all those gathered. Then Jesus asked an unexpected question: *Do you want to be made well?* (v. 6).

What kind of question was that for someone who had been sick longer than most people in his generation had been alive? This man probably had prayed more prayers than we can imagine and had sought every kind of help that was available to him, including putting his faith in this bubbling water. Surely there had been enough desperation to call for ten miracles!

But it's not always a given that we want to get well. Jesus knows to ask because unless we are partners in our own healing by relying more on Jesus than we have on the limited world in which we've lived in the past, we will return to captivity—whether it's the same or another kind.

Do you want to be made well? The question reminds us that sometimes our brokenness becomes home to us, making the hardship of the past seem safer than the unknowns of freedom that lie ahead. What would it mean for this man to be made well? He'd have to become responsible for his life, invest fully in relationships instead of being passively cared for, work for his food, and participate fully in the world. His broken state, as hard as it had been, may have seemed to be a comfortable, known world of safety— and less risky than a new and unknown life outside the walls of sickness.

The Gospel of John tells us that his healing happened on the Sabbath. This is an important detail. The Sabbath is a day of rest given to us as a gift from God. God rested on the seventh day of Creation not because he was tired—after all, an all-powerful God can't be tired—but because he wanted to model for his people what completion or wholeness looks like. When Creation was complete or whole, God stepped back and sanctified it with a day that was set apart from the others.

So, one reason for Sabbath rest is to recognize God's sovereignty as the Creator over creation, which includes you and me. Later in Scripture, when God's people were reminded to keep the Sabbath, it was a way for them to remember this. Even today, when we are tempted to find our identity in our work or our hurried lifestyles, Sabbath reminds us that we are so much more in God's eyes: we are his beloved creations.

A second reason for Sabbath rest was to commemorate the Exodus, when God freed his people from the bondage of slavery in Egypt. When God's people were slaves, they could not take a day to rest or worship. Now a day of rest for all households—including servants—would remind them that they had been freed from tyranny and should model God's loving-kindness to others.

Even though Sabbath was a gift meant to provide rest and assurance of God's love, over time God's people made it a rule rather than a celebration. In fact, they made rules about how to follow the rules! Instead of finding joy and peace in the Sabbath, God's people often associated it with fear and legalism as they tried to decide exactly what the rule of Sabbath prohibited them from doing.

When Jesus healed on the Sabbath, the rule-enforcing Pharisees found themselves in a dilemma. On one hand, they observed Jesus doing "work," which was prohibited. On the other hand, the healings that the crowds witnessed on these Sabbath days were clearly acts of the kind of *shalom* (peace) and wholeness that were compatible with God's original vision for Sabbath.

Sabbath is a vision of wholeness and restoration, and Jesus beautifully embodied that vision when he healed people on the Sabbath. His healings celebrated God's recreating of his world by healing the broken and making all things new. His healings also broke the bondage of sickness and death and restored freedom to those who received healing.

When the man was healed, Jesus commanded him to get up, carry his mat, and walk. The Jewish leaders—those who were very invested in making and enforcing rules about how to keep the Sabbath—found that the man was walking around with his mat, and they were upset. Clearly it was against the law to carry burdens on the Sabbath, and carrying a mat could be interpreted as work.

Jesus's act of healing on the Sabbath, which embodied God's grace and love, stands in stark contrast to the religious leaders' concerns about doing work on the Sabbath—evidence of their cold and rigid practice of religion. Jesus lifted the man's burden of sickness and commanded him to pick up the very thing he had laid on all of his life in despair. The Jewish teachers were offended to find him carrying his mat, showing that they cared more about rules than about the man's healing. Their way of seeing God's law only burdened the man, while Jesus's gift of healing set him free.

When offended Jewish teachers asked the man who had given him this law-breaking command to carry his mat, he didn't even know Jesus's identity! I love the idea that people can be touched by God before they even realize who God is.

The man had one more chance to learn who Jesus was when he met him later in the temple. Jesus instructed the man to stop sinning so that nothing worse may happen to him. Odd words after such a gracious and mercy-filled act of healing, right?

I find it interesting how often Jesus connected physical healing with references to the problem of sin and freedom from sin. Jesus was not saying that the man's sin had caused his sickness; rather, he recognized that as burdened as the man had been from physical problems, the sin in his life would burden him even more if he did not find a new way of living for God. Sin can cause something worse than physical illness because it can be spiritually fatal. Jesus wanted this man to be healed and whole in body *and* spirit, and he wouldn't stop "stirring up" the waters of his life until the man was restored to the way God intended in Creation.

In all of these healing stories, we see a common denominator: Jesus's compassion. Jesus is moved to act out of his deep compassion for broken and hurting people. God wants nothing but the best for you—nothing short of your wholeness and restoration. God's goal is the complete restoration and wholeness of his creation, of which you are a treasured part! Know that Jesus's desire for your complete wholeness is a part of a grander picture that will restore the world to the beauty and completeness of Eden. He loves you and the rest of creation so much that nothing will stand in his way!

CHAPTER 5

A Two-for-One Miracle Story

The Power of True Love

Our kids have recently turned six and eight years old, and my husband and I feel we have a major parenting challenge and responsibility: how and when to introduce them to the greatest movies of all time. We've seen *The Wizard of Oz, Mary Poppins*, the original Muppet movie, and *Annie*. But what should be next?

I was sure it needed to be what I consider a classic, a combination of adventure tale, love story, and comedy: *The Princess Bride*.

If you're not familiar with it, let me give you a quick introduction. A boy is home sick for the day. And his grandfather comes over to read to him an adventure book that the grandfather used to read to the boy's father when he was sick. The boy asks if it has any sports in it, and the grandfather says, "Are you kidding? Fencing, fighting, torture, revenge, giants, monsters, chases, escapes, true love, miracles." The little boy thinks that doesn't sound too bad and says he'll try to stay awake.

The grandfather begins the story telling how a girl named Buttercup was raised on a small farm in the country and enjoyed riding her horse and tormenting Westley, the boy who worked on the farm. She would issue a command, and his response was always, "As you wish." One day when he answered "as you wish," she realized that he really meant "I love you." And she was even more amazed when she realized she loved him too.

Now in the next scene, she and Westley draw close to kiss. And we hear the little boy saying, "Hold it, hold it. What is this? Are you trying to trick me? Where's the sports? Is this a kissing story?"[1]

Another thing I love about this movie is that it's like two movies in one. There's this story about a boy who is sick in bed, who would rather play video games than listen to his grandfather read to him from some old book, and an old man who loves his grandson and would love to win his heart by reading him one of the greatest stories ever written. You're just barely into this story when the second movie starts. There's this story about a girl who loves a boy and all the obstacles that get in the way of their being together—a story about true love and giants and sword fighting and revenge. It's like a movie within a movie, a story within a story.

A story technique called framing is used, when you set one story inside another one like a picture inside a frame. And when this kind of story is told really well, each of the stories adds to the other one and helps bring it to light. The frame illuminates the beauty of the picture, and the picture brings out the beauty of the frame. We see this kind of framing—a story within a story—in the Gospel of Mark.

Two Healings, One Message

In Mark 5, we see two healings within one story. Jesus gets summoned to the bedside of a dying girl, and on his way to save her, another woman jockeys her way to get close enough to some of Jesus's healing power. The relationship between these two healings and the reasons they are paired in the Gospel of Mark are not only fascinating; they actually reveal the message in all of God's miracles: *God longs to show us his true and perfect love.*

These two miracles take place one day as Jesus is in the midst of a large crowd that is pressing in around him. A religious leader named Jairus rushes in to beg for Jesus's help because his daughter is sick and dying. As Jesus is on his way to help, a woman who is very sick reaches out and touches his cloak in order to seek healing. These two events don't seem to be connected. Jairus does not know the woman and has never had any contact with her. But these two stories tell us even more together than they would have separately.[2] Let's consider seven significant similarities they share to understand about God's longing to show us his perfect love.

1. The Time Frame

Even if you are familiar with these two stories in Mark 5, it's likely that you have never noticed or paid much attention to this particular similarity. But as it turns out, this small detail is anything but insignificant.

The age of Jairus's daughter and the length of the woman's illness were the same: twelve years. This small detail is actually a major connection between the two stories. The severity of the woman's condition is made even clearer by the fact that she has been ill for as long as the little girl has been alive! We have already established the importance of the number twelve, as Israel was organized into twelve tribes descended from the twelve sons of Jacob (Genesis 49), and Jesus's followers mirrored that number as twelve disciples. The connection in these healing stories to the twelve tribes and the twelve disciples reminds us of Jesus's desire to heal not only individual bodies but also the people of God as a corporate body. God loves us individually and listens to the cries of our hearts, but he's also focusing on a bigger picture than we could ever imagine, gathering a people to himself and working on the restoration of all of creation.

2. The Threat of Death

Another similarity we see in both stories is the threat of death. The first thing we learn from Jairus is the seriousness of his daughter's condition.

Clearly Jairus's little girl is dying, and he is desperate to get Jesus to her before death claims her as a victim. Similarly, the condition of the bleeding woman is certainly leading her on a trajectory toward death. She has lost blood continually for twelve long years, and nothing she has tried has stopped the bleeding.

Anyone who heard about this woman's plight with continual bleeding would have associated her story with death. The Old Testament emphasizes again and again the nature of blood as the "life fluid" of a living being, so it was only a matter of time before her life would be drained from her body through the loss of her blood. Both she and Jairus were fighting for life, and Jesus was the only One who could help them.

3. The Presence of Noise, Chaos, and Commotion

Another common denominator of these two stories is the commotion in which they take place. Where there is a crowd, you can be sure there is commotion! There is not only a noisy, turbulent crowd surrounding Jesus when both Jairus and the bleeding woman approach him but also a crowd waiting at Jairus's house.

When Jesus finally arrives at Jairus's home, there is quite a commotion there too. A crowd of mourners has gathered, and there is loud crying and wailing. It's possible that these mourners were not even family or friends but were paid mourners, as was the custom. From beginning to end of both stories, we find noise, chaos, and commotion.

4. The Presence of Fear

Still another commonality between the stories of Jairus and the bleeding woman is fear, which we see in their postures before Jesus. Within a few verses of each other, both of these figures are kneeling before Jesus. We read that Jairus "begged him repeatedly" (v. 23), which suggests desperation caused by anxiety and fear. As a parent, I can only imagine how desperate he must have felt. It's intriguing that while Jairus is afraid on the front end of his miracle, the bleeding woman's fear is mentioned after she is healed—at the discovery of what she has done.

Jesus calms the fear present in both of them with his actions and his words. He says to the woman, "Go in peace" (v. 34), and to Jairus, "Do not fear, only believe" (v. 36). Jesus's presence always overwhelms and extinguishes the presence of fear.

5. The Presence of Faith

Just as we see the presence of fear in both stories, so we see the presence of faith. It took great faith for the woman to approach Jesus—even to sneak up on him for a secret healing. It also took faith for Jairus, a leader in the religious community, to come to Jesus so publicly with his needs—and even more faith to continue to trust Jesus after he found out that his daughter had died.

Both of these individuals lived with faith and fear at the same time. They remind us that sometimes we will feel both at once. Jesus doesn't need us to overcome fear on our own; he wants us to bring what little faith we have to him so that he can help us with our fears.

6. "Immediately"

These two stories also share an important word that is found many times in Mark's Gospel: *immediately*. "Immediately her hemorrhage stopped; and she felt in her body that she was healed of her disease" (v. 29). "And immediately the girl got up and began to walk about" (v. 42).

With these healings, we're talking about moving from death to life, from broken to whole in an instant. Neither the girl nor the woman had to wait another second to see if Jesus's healing "took." When Jesus reaches out to heal these two individuals, there is no delay.

While not all of our needs or requests are remedied immediately, the use of this word in these stories emphasizes Jesus's power to heal. These healing stories show us the heart of Jesus. He was moved by Jairus' request, and he was moved to stop the crowd and find the woman who had reached out to him. Jesus walked around with healing power at the ready, and that same power is offered to us even still today. And while our total healing may or may not come immediately as it did for them, we can be sure that we will experience a kind of peace and calm when we put our trust in Jesus.

7. The Return of Peace and Calm

Look closely and you'll see that both healings end with peace and calm. Even in the midst of the chaotic crowd, Jesus calmly seeks to give his attention to one inconspicuous woman. As we've already seen, he tells her to "go in peace" (v. 34), a state very different from the way she entered the scene. Jesus is reassuring her that she has done nothing wrong in seeking healing and that he graciously gives what she has taken from him.

Later, when Jesus reaches Jairus's house, he drives the noisy mourners away before he goes to encounter the little girl (v. 40). When Jesus brings their daughter back to life, it restores peace and joy to the household.

These two human beings—the religious leader Jairus and the woman with a bleeding disorder—really had nothing in common. If they had met on the street on an average day, they wouldn't have spoken to each other. It's likely they wouldn't even have walked down the same street! But they are united by these common experiences of suffering, fear, and desperation before Jesus. Their stories are also united by the ability of Jesus to heal and restore, respond to their needs with compassion and grace, and change their world in a heartbeat. Jesus is so kind. We even hear his kindness audibly in his voice as he calls to both the young girl and the bleeding woman, addressing them both affectionately with the same word, *daughter*.

"Daughter"

It is significant that in both healings Jesus used the word *daughter*. With this one word, Jesus made it personal. He was giving an invitation into a relationship. That's the end game of compassion: relationship. Because of Jesus's compassion for us—his great love for us—his desire is for a relationship with us. Jesus used the word *daughter* to pronounce the bleeding woman healed, whole, loved, treasured, blessed. It's the same word a father, like Jairus, would use to talk about a treasured child. Jairus was a named leader in the synagogue, a man of power and privilege with the resources of connections and community. He was a father in deep pain because of his profound love for his gravely ill daughter.

While it may be common today for a family to have one child, in Jairus's culture it was the hope of each family to have many children— especially sons. Sons were a source of investment and stability, a way to make sure that the parents were taken care of in their old age and that their business would be passed down. The more sons a family had, the better off they would be in the long run. A daughter would leave and join her husband's family upon marrying—something that was not too distant for a twelve-year-old daughter who would be coming of age very soon. So Jairus's reaction to his daughter's illness shows a love that goes beyond seeing her as an asset or possession or even as a liability, as women were often seen in those days. His love for her is emotional and personal. She is precious to him.

Because Jairus was a man of respect and position, it would be considered improper for him to beg. So it is shocking for him to press through the common masses of people gathered around Jesus, shout to get Jesus's attention (as he surely had to do), fall at Jesus's feet, and beg repeatedly.

Apart from our two-for-one story, there is only one other instance in the Gospel of Mark where someone falls at Jesus's feet—the Syrophoenician woman in chapter 7.

Like the Syrophoenician woman, Jairus's love for his little daughter, who was precious to him, meant that he cared more for her than his own dignity and standing in society. He lowered himself to beg at the feet of a renegade rabbi, whose teaching and presence in Jairus's community was probably scandalous—including in the very synagogue where Jairus was a leader. Love for a child can make someone cross all boundaries and give up everything if she or he believes it can help that child. Jairus is living proof of that. And Jesus responded with compassionate love, agreeing to go with Jairus, even in the face of the worst news this father could have received.

While Jairus is named, we never learn the bleeding woman's name. While Jairus was privileged, having status and connections in the community, she was alone and full of shame. Even her approach to Jesus seems to make her merely a disruption in a more important man's story—an inconvenient interruption when the life of a precious daughter was on the line.

This woman's story is one some people are uncomfortable with because of the nature of her disease: bleeding for twelve years. If some can be uncomfortable naming it even today, then we have only a small view of what those in her own culture experienced. Her illness was no ordinary malady that would have allowed her family or community to surround her with care and help. In fact, there were laws devoted to women who were bleeding—not only as part of a regular menstrual cycle (see Leviticus 15:19) but also as an ongoing condition.

Because of the nature of her illness, this woman was not only sick but also completely isolated. She lived alone and could not touch anyone. If she had a husband, and perhaps even a child, she would not have been able to have lived with or touched them in twelve years.

This desperate woman had tried everything to cure her illness, including spending *all* of her money and resources on doctors. But the attempted cures of primitive medicine might have been worse than the condition itself, because we're told that she only grew worse.

She knew better than to be in a crowd like this. The Jews considered her uncleanness contagious, and if anyone touched her, they would be spiritually and physically unclean too. If anyone in that crowd recognized her as stepping out of her rightful place, she would be revealed as putting the multitudes in danger and ostracized—perhaps even beaten or stoned.

Why would she take a risk like this? To put it very simply, she was desperate. She had *nothing* left to lose. She was beyond all hope and had exhausted every resource available to her. She must have heard about Jesus the healer, and she knew he was her last chance.

While Jesus was on his way to help Jairus, she struggled through the crowd, got just close enough to this holy man, and reached out with her unclean hand to touch the most remote part of him possible—the outermost piece of his clothing. Suddenly her body must have felt amazingly different and restored; the exhaustion, pain, and illness she had suffered for so long had flooded out of her and had been replaced by a powerful sense of wholeness and well-being. Jesus's cleanness had been more contagious than her uncleanness, and a mere touch brought restoration to her body. At the same time, she was terrified because Jesus was looking around him. "Who touched me?" He asked as he scanned the faces closest to him.

She had shoplifted her healing—stolen power from the great I AM—and now he wanted to know who had done it.

What a terrifying feeling to know that someone so powerful could turn that power on you in a destructive way if that person chose to!

Unlike Jairus, who was someone of high status as a leader in the synagogue, this woman was a nobody. Being both a woman and someone with a spiritually unclean disease meant that she was not supposed to approach someone like Jesus for help. Yet both she and Jairus had come to the end of themselves and had nowhere else to turn. Desperation is the great equalizer. It puts all of us at the feet of Jesus, asking for his help.

Jairus's answered prayer happened in a private home away from questioning eyes. The bleeding woman's healing happened in a very public place where she never wanted to be noticed. I wonder if the "whole truth" she told Jesus included the story of her illness, shame, isolation, and exhaustion. I wonder how much of it Jesus knew by just looking in her eyes. But instead of responding in anger, he looked down at her with compassion and spoke the word that changed her life forever.

Jesus called her *daughter*. How long had it been since anyone called her that—or spoke any word with kindness? This man, whose touch and words everyone was clamoring for, took time to look into her eyes. He took time to hear her "whole truth." He stopped the entire entourage—the surging crowd and the disciples whispering that he needed to hurry up because they were urgently on their way somewhere important to heal the daughter of a VIP who was dying. *She* was important enough for him to stop everything.

Daughter. We've already heard that word spoken by a man who deeply loved his child. And Jairus's way of loving has shown us just what that word can mean: that a father could love a daughter enough that she was treasured beyond any value or collateral the world assigned to her; that a father could deem a daughter so valuable that he would leave his high position and lower himself if it meant she might be saved; that he would give anything if it meant sparing her life. The way Jairus felt about his little princess, his only daughter in the world who was so young that life for her had not really yet begun, is the way Jesus felt about this woman, who had been cast off by the world as if she had no value and dismissed as if her life was near the end.

Daughter. With that one word, Jesus told her she was worth everything to him. For twelve years Jairus's daughter had been treasured, loved, and spoiled. For twelve years this woman had been outcast, scorned, and rejected. One was cradled while the other was untouched. "Now," Jesus said, "you will know that you are treasured too. You are more than just healed; you are my daughter. Go in peace."

We long to hear these words too. We long for relationship with our loving God, and the good news is that he longs for it as well. We are treasured and loved by the God who sees and knows all of our hurts, visible and hidden, and loves us with more compassion than we could ever imagine. In fact, his love is so great for us that he calls us his children. God calls us all sons and daughters.

The Sting of Death

In our two-for-one miracle story, we've seen not only the threat of death but the *reality* of death. Jairus' daughter actually dies, and people gathered at her house begin to mourn her loss. The sting of death is actually a real thing—it hurts when people we love die. It hurts when we grieve the loss of those we love.

I'll never forget the very first funeral that I presided over as a pastor. I stood in the pulpit, looking out over a sea of grieving, tear-streaked faces, and read this passage from First Corinthians:

"Death has been swallowed up in victory."
"Where, O death, is your victory?
Where, O death, is your sting?" (15:54-55)

I remember thinking, *What a ridiculous question!* These people know exactly where the sting of death is. They are hurting from it right now. The person they love is gone, and they would do anything to bring her back.

The ultimate power Jesus exhibits over death is resurrection, the fundamental reversal of death itself.

Besides presiding as a pastor before other families who have felt cheated by death, I've stood myself where they stand. I've felt the deep pain and loss for family members gone too soon, most memorably my younger cousin Brian, who died tragically at twenty-one-years-old the day before Christmas Eve. As any family who's had a time of shock and deep loss can attest, that anniversary and the memory of Brian's loss will always be a part of our Christmas memories. The sting of death, even with healing over the years, is still remembered, especially on that day each year.

The sting of death has driven all of us to desperate places. Loss and grief are some of the most common elements of the human experience, and yet when we go through them, it seems as if no one else can understand the depth of our pain.

But Jesus understands the depth of our pain. He experienced the loss of those closest to him: his cousin John the Baptist was brutally killed by a tyrant, and we know his own earthly father Joseph probably died sometime in Jesus's youth or young adulthood, since he is not present in any Gospel stories past Jesus's twelfth year. When we witness Jesus's own witnessing of death and loss, we see a heart filled with human compassion. We also see a God who loves his children so much that he will do anything to take down the adversary of death.

While we watch Jesus in isolated battles with death throughout his ministry, there is a greater war being waged. God began the world as a place where death had no place in the unspoiled creation that was his perfect will. So, in order to return his people to a place with no more death or mourning or crying or pain (Revelation 21:4), Jesus undertook a comprehensive campaign of war against death itself!

Actually, death is not just a single event experienced once in each of our lives. Dr. Joseph Dongell imagines death as an octopus, operating multiple tentacles to draw prey toward destruction.[3] According to this picture, while we may not always recognize these different facets as being tentacles or extensions of death's scheme, they are unified and cooperative, under the control of a single power. He suggests that the major tentacles of death are: Satan and his demons; human structures of injustice, evil, violence, and warfare; sin itself, with its own corrupting and corrosive effects; sickness and disease of all kinds (including mental illnesses and addictions); human ignorance, both in general and in relation to God's truth and love; and nature turned destructive (for example, storms, earthquakes, volcanoes, drought, fire, flood).[4]

Death is the ultimate goal or outcome of each of these tentacles or schemes—though it is easier to recognize in some of them than in others.

All lead toward the destruction of people, relationships, and communities and therefore are the tools of death itself.

In the Scriptures we see Jesus doing everything in his power to combat each of these extensions of death and ultimately reach his final goal: to destroy death itself. He demonstrates power to overcome all of these tentacles through casting out evil spirits, justice, forgiveness, healing, teaching, and rescue.

All of these powerful acts are ways that Jesus battles the enemy of death. Of course, the ultimate power Jesus exhibits over death is resurrection, the *reversal* of death itself. Jesus's own resurrection from the tomb is the culmination of his ministry on earth. It shows us that he has broken the power of death itself and now makes a way for us to live with him eternally.

The moment Jesus healed the bleeding woman must have been such an amazing moment of surprise, joy, and relief. The moment Jesus took the hand of Jairus's little girl and helped her rise from her deathbed must have been the most astonishing and joyful moment of her parents' lives!

Jesus opposes the tentacles of death at every turn. With every miracle, he strikes another blow against his opponent. But he knows that the only thing that will bring the decisive upset will be his own death—and then the defeat of death through his resurrection. While he could have gone on raising person after person from the grave, the truth is that each person would eventually die again. He knew that if he actually entered death himself and won, he would defeat the enemy that faces each of us and be able to bring us into eternity with him, where death no longer has power over us.

I know what it's like to mourn the loss of someone I love. You do too. Death is a part of all our lives, and it's sometimes hard to remember the deep truths of God when the sting of death is so personal and so fresh. But the words of 1 Corinthians 15 can help remind us of Jesus's victory until we all can say them together in eternity. Whether I'm presiding over a funeral or reading the words to myself in my own time of need, I say them with confidence yet also with compassion, acknowledging that we can say what is true even if we don't yet *feel* it at the time. We can say it because he fought death for us, and won!

> "Death has been swallowed up in victory."
> "Where, O death, is your victory?
> Where, O death, is your sting?"
> The sting of death is sin, and the power of sin is the law. But thanks be to God, who gives us the victory through our Lord Jesus Christ. (1 Corinthians 15:54-57)

These words remind us that while death may sting for a moment, we can be assured that the final victory is won. Earthly deaths feel like a sting, but they will pale in comparison to the joyful reunions in eternity. In his great compassion and love for us, Jesus took on death and won so that we could live with him forever. Thank God, Jesus never tires of showing compassion.

Jesus's Compassion

I'm captivated by works of art that depict Jesus. Seeing Jesus's face reflected in paintings or stained glass or even modern art installations makes me study his expression a little closer and wonder, *What side of Jesus did the artist want us to see? How is Jesus feeling in this moment? If this portrait could speak, what would Jesus say?* Every single portrait is different, and each one is an artist's representation of what he or she believed about Jesus. Was he serious? Angry or upset? Sometimes he is smiling or looking amused. A handful of times, I have seen Jesus depicted as laughing. Yet, although we know it happened, I can't even think of one occasion when I've seen a painting of Jesus crying.

Jesus was filled with emotion. his interactions with people show deeply held feelings and wonderfully personal reactions. When I picture Jesus in the middle of healing the bleeding woman and raising Jairus's daughter from the dead, I can't imagine a wooden, unfeeling Jesus speaking his lines as if they were written on cue cards. When Jesus saw Jairus's reaction at the news that his daughter had died or locked eyes with the woman in the crowd, he *felt* for them. His heart was tender, and he was filled with compassion. He connected with their emotions, felt empathy, and offered his best to reach their worst.

God heals because he loves. He created our world in love, and now he lovingly works to restore the brokenness of his creation. When Jesus healed, he engaged in great acts of power. But healing is not ultimately about power. Healing is about love.[5]

The Greek word often used to describe Jesus's compassion is *splanchnizomai*. (If you say it out loud, someone may respond with "God bless you!") It means "to be affected deeply in one's inner being (bowels)."[6]

This kind of compassion will not be still. It evokes a response. Every time someone in the Gospels is described as having this kind of compassion, they are moved. Literally, they move toward the one they feel compassion for, and that person responds.

Jesus feels and acts on compassion by moving toward the people in deep need that he encounters. Before many of the miracles, he displays or is described as having this compassion that leads to action. The deep emotion that Jesus feels when he encounters desperation leads him to act in power.

Jesus cares for the crowds but also sees the needs of an individual that he can help, and he zeroes in on the person's desperation as he works toward a solution. We see exactly this side of Jesus in the story of Jairus's daughter and the outcast woman Jesus honors with the name *daughter*. When Jairus falls at Jesus's feet in desperation, looking for help for his dying daughter, Jesus immediately leaves the crowd and goes with him. And when the woman touches Jesus's cloak, and he feels power leave him, he stops everything to find her in the crowd and takes time to hear her story. Instead of just curing her, Jesus heals her. He speaks life to her, including declaring publicly that she is well—a priestly statement that would restore her to her family and community.

Compassion cares for the crowds, but when there is an individual who has a deep and desperate need, compassion is not afraid to turn and focus energy and resources and love until that need is heard and cared for.

You are more than a number in a crowd to Jesus. When he sees your anguish and pain, he has this kind of moving compassion for you. It's more than a feeling; it results in action—the action of God's grace and mercy expressed in your life.

When you feel compassion toward others, you can recall these stories and mirror the look you imagine in Jesus's eyes in these instances. You can see the individuals instead of letting them get lost in the crowd. You can ask questions about their feelings and needs. And you can pray for them.

Sometimes we pray for people, but they are not physically healed. But through prayer they always receive Jesus's compassion. Prayer is one of the best ways to show love and compassion for someone. It carries the ones we love to the One whose compassion moves heaven and earth. We may not have the ability to heal or restore, but we can participate in God's act of healing others when we pray for their healing. We can show compassion to others and participate in the compassion that God pours out so generously on us all. We can carry others into the arms of the Healer when they lack the strength themselves. Healing stories show us that God's compassion is for all of us—no matter the depth of our need or where we come from.

Compassion for All

Countless lives were touched by Jesus's healing miracles, but healing was always more than an individual gift. The healings of Christ were also confirmation of his compassionate plan for *all* of God's people—God's plan to redeem the world through Christ.

We know from Matthew's Gospel that Jesus's cousin John the Baptist was in prison (11:2), and word was getting back to John about Jesus's miraculous actions. Picking up the story in the Gospel of Luke, we learn that John sent a couple of his own disciples to ask Jesus, "Are you the one who is to come, or should we expect someone else?" (Luke 7:18-20 NIV). What did he mean by "Are you the one who is to come?"

John's entire ministry has been preparing the way for the Messiah, the One who would come to rescue God's people. John had spent his life telling people about the Messiah. There had been some wonderful clues that these hopes were being fulfilled in his younger cousin, Jesus. He had witnessed the Spirit of the Lord descend on Jesus when he baptized him. He had pointed the way to Jesus and declared: "Look, the Lamb of God, who takes away the sin of the world!" (John 1:29 NIV). And yet, he still had to ask, "Are you the one? Are you the Messiah?"

I can imagine John, unjustly imprisoned and knowing that he would probably die there behind the prison walls yet reaching out to Jesus. John had offended a king who was known for his erratic and cruel actions, and the outlook for his survival was not good. He wanted to know at the end of his life and ministry if he had been right about Jesus. He also was hearing remarkable stories about Jesus's miraculous actions and needed to know firsthand if they were true—if they were signs that the Messiah had finally come to rescue God's people.

When John asks, "Are you the one?" Jesus sends back a message. He tells John's disciples to report what they have witnessed, what they have personally seen and heard (Luke 7:22).

Jesus indeed had care and compassion for individuals, but these healings also were a sign that the kingdom of God was breaking into the kingdom of this world and defeating the signs of evil, sin, and death.

John the Baptist himself had preached a message about the nearness of the kingdom of God. He traveled around the wilderness of Judea proclaiming, "Repent, for the kingdom of heaven has come near" (Matthew 3:2).

While we recognize signs—including the miracles of Jesus—as indications that the kingdom of God is present in our midst, another reality is that God's kingdom is not yet fully here. We call this the paradox of "already/not yet." Understanding that Jesus is already Lord of this world but that the world does not yet look or function as God wants it to, helps us understand things like healing. We know not everyone will be healed in our "not yet" world. We know that not everything will look or function the way God wants it to. We know that we will find ourselves desperate for Jesus to work a miracle. But we are looking forward to a day when we can proclaim the triumphant words of Revelation 11:15, which are included in George Frideric Handel's "Hallelujah Chorus": "The kingdom of this world is become the kingdom of our Lord, and of his Christ."

Healing comes in many forms, but it is always a confirmation of God's care and compassion for all of us. His presence is with us no matter our circumstances. Healing is also a sign that God's kingdom is both here and on its way in fullness. God's love for you is greater than any circumstance or struggle you are going through. His love is a rescuing, healing love, and he has declared his overwhelming love for *you*.

Jesus shows us that nothing, not even death, can stop him. He'll show us that again at the cross if we'll just stay with him—that no obstacle will get between God and his children that he loves with such compassionate tenderness, that true love can't be stopped by any obstacle—not by devastating medical news, isolation or loneliness, crushing debt, anxiety, or worry. Not even death can stop Jesus from his kids. He'll go through even the worst for us. And he'll do it even for those who consider themselves the least worthy.

We can come to Jesus again and again with unanswered prayers and broken hearts. We can come to Jesus when we have felt ourselves outside of the circle of his attention. We can ask Jesus to look us in the eyes again and call us by that healing word, *daughter* or *son*. We can pray that Jesus would show us the depth of his love and show us that true love can overcome any obstacle.

That's what this two-for-one miracle story is about—the big story of a Father's compassionate, tender love that's too deep to be stopped by any obstacle even when the biggest obstacle to our being loved is ourselves. It's the story of a Father who will stop at nothing to save his kids—the story of obstacles, brokenness, sickness and death, and how nothing could hold him back. True love is unstoppable, and that's the greatest miracle, the greatest story of all.

CHAPTER 6

THE GRAND MIRACLE

JESUS HIMSELF

A pastor was thumbing through the prayer request cards people had dropped in the offering plates that Sunday and found one written by a ten-year-old:

> Dear Jesus, thank you for keeping us in your loving heart. Thank you for giving all of these different miracles from learning to ride your bike to putting footsteps on the moon. We thank you for giving us food to eat and fresh water to drink. You do so much for us that we can't thank you back. You are my miracle. Amen. (Alex, Age 10)

Alex must have had miracles on his mind that day. He wanted to thank God for the simplest act that seemed like a miracle to him—learning to ride a bike—and the most awe-inspiring—walking on the moon. He recognized that there was way more to thank God for than he could begin to mention. But then he mentioned one thing that seemed to capture all the blessings into one. I can't get over the simple and profound way that he put it: "You are my miracle."

It's true, isn't it? Jesus himself is a miracle. The very existence and identity of God who became human, who walked and laughed and ate and slept and stubbed his toe, all of that is itself a singular miracle.

In this chapter, we'll look at the miracles of Jesus through the lens of the miracle that is Jesus himself.

The Miracle of Incarnation

The miracle of Jesus's identity as both fully God and fully human is called the *Incarnation*. It's one of the simplest truths of the Christian faith yet possibly one of the hardest to wrap our minds around.

In Jesus, God and humanity have become one. How can this even be possible? To define God is to paint categories that are outside of human possibility. He is without limits in his knowledge (omniscience), location (omnipresence), and power (omnipotence). As humans, we are all too aware of our own limits in those categories and many more.

While we often accept the truth of Jesus's identity without question, it can be one of the hardest truths to understand or explain. Ben Witherington, one of the brightest biblical scholars I know, says so: "Incarnation is not something that human beings can fully get their mental calipers around. It involves miracle and mystery, and is frankly above our mental pay grade, even for the brightest amongst us."[1]

Yet my five-year-old daughter and my ninety-six-year-old grandmother both grasp the truth of Jesus's identity with ease. They both adore Jesus, talk about him with a familiarity, and revere him as holy. Both of them are my teachers as I seek to understand more about having a relationship with Jesus, because they both approach him with a simplicity that is effortless. Ask my daughter if Jesus is God, and her answer is yes. Ask her if Jesus is a person, and you'll get the same answer: yes. Jesus makes sense to her even before she can spell his name.

When an angel appeared to Mary and announced her role in the

Incarnation, she had trouble grasping just what was going to happen. Most of us would have too! But God comforted and assured her of his presence and his purposes.

From the beginning, God's incarnation was tough to grapple with, but his promises were reassurances of his presence, his favor, and his success. The angel told Mary that "nothing will be impossible with God" (Luke 1:37 NASB); the New International Version says, "No word from God will ever fail." Jesus would be the very Word of God (John 1:1). This crazy-sounding plan of the unification of God and man would be a success. As we read in John 1:14, "The Word became flesh and lived among us, and we have seen his glory, the glory as of a father's only son, full of grace and truth."

The Greek word for "lived among us" or "dwelt among us" is *skenoo*, literally meaning "to pitch a tent."[2] This verse could be translated, "The Word became flesh and pitched his tent in our camp alongside our tents." God was taking on the tent of flesh and neurons and skin cells and taste buds and muscle fibers and DNA. And with all the great things about the human condition, he also was pledging to take on influenza and chicken pox and grief and rejection and pain and, ultimately, death.

God's people had traveled in the wilderness with a tabernacle where God lived among them (Exodus 40:34-35), so this concept of God in a tent was nothing new. Only this time the tent God would inhabit was a human being, who would encounter every temptation and trial that can come to the human nature. God was taking on the struggles we have as human beings along with our DNA.

In early Christianity, as people were working out what the church believed and how to understand difficult truths, most of the major heresies—beliefs contrary to what the church came to accept as truth—centered around misunderstandings of who Jesus was. As people tried to explain Jesus's identity, they tipped too far to one side or the other—either believing that "Jesus was so fully God that he really wasn't human after all but was just occupying a human container," or that "Jesus was so human that he wasn't fully God but just a person that God made." Some people were unbalanced in their understanding of the Incarnation, but the church insisted that Jesus was 100 percent God and 100 percent human all at once.

Clarity on the identity and life of Jesus was one of the main reasons the church established the creeds. The Apostles' Creed states what we believe about God the Father in two lines ("I believe in God the Father Almighty, / maker of heaven and earth") and what we believe about the Holy Spirit in one simple line: "I believe in the Holy Spirit."[3] It doesn't get much simpler than that! Yet what we believe about Jesus is retold in *ten* lines:

> I believe in Jesus Christ, his only Son, our Lord,
>> who was conceived by the Holy Spirit,
>> born of the Virgin Mary,
>> suffered under Pontius Pilate,
>> was crucified, died, and was buried;
>> he descended to the dead.
>> On the third day he rose again;
>> he ascended into heaven,
>> is seated at the right hand of the Father,
>> and will come again to judge the living and the dead.[4]

So much space is given to Jesus in the creed not because one member of the Trinity is more important than others but because there were many misunderstandings in early Christianity about Jesus that needed balancing and clarifying. Getting our arms around the truth about Jesus's life and identity is important for the church, and it's just as important to our study of miracles.

All other miracles exist to point us
to relationship with the One who
is our miracle.

C. S. Lewis put it this way: "The central miracle asserted by Christians is the Incarnation. They say that God became Man. Every other miracle prepares for this, or exhibits this, or results from this. . . . The fitness, and therefore credibility, of the particular miracles depends on their relation to the Grand Miracle; all discussion of them in isolation from it is futile."[5]

The Grand Miracle. I like that phrase. The Grand Miracle is that God became flesh and lived among us. The "particular miracles" that Jesus does, as Lewis calls them, are all meant to point to the Miracle of miracles, the Grand Miracle that is Jesus.We've read the stories of the miracles Jesus performed, but the greatest—the grandest—miracle of all is that God bent low to become one of us and pave a road back to him.

God Bent Low

I love the imagery in the phrase *God bent low*. Just thinking about how the God of the universe, seated high in the heavens above, loves us so much that he came down to know us, to save us, and to show us what he means by his love. The carols we sing at Christmas all point to this beautiful truth that God bends low, from heaven to earth in a quiet but grand way.

The weeks leading up to Christmas are always a season of expectation and preparation. It's certainly true in my house as I'm sure it is in yours. We look forward to gatherings, plan for parties, shop for gifts, and decorate as if our lives depend on it! With all the emphasis on preparation, I sometimes start to believe that Christmas depends on me. I catch myself thinking that if I will just do all the right things ahead of time, Christmas will turn out perfectly. Have you ever had similar thoughts? Sometimes, no matter how much we prepare, Christmas turns out differently than we expected.

What happens when Christmas throws us a curveball? What does it mean when our celebrations aren't perfect but are messy, unexpected, and surprising in all the wrong ways?

We need to keep in mind that Christmas was a miracle precisely *because* it was unexpected. God's people had been waiting for a Messiah to come for so long that they had gotten their hopes up very high. They imagined great things about the Messiah: that he would be strong and powerful, a commanding political leader as the world had never known. When they anticipated his birth, they knew that a mighty king, of course, would be born in a palace, wrapped in the finest cloths, and placed in a fancy bed.

But that's certainly not what the Messiah's first visitors found. They found a poor family in a borrowed space intended for animals. Max Lucado paints it this way: "Majesty in the midst of the mundane. Holiness in the filth of sheep manure and sweat. Divinity entering the world on the floor of a stable, through the womb of a teenager and in the presence of a carpenter."[6]

If the shepherds had come with assumptions about how a king should enter the world, they might have rejected the simple baby they found lying in an animal's feeding trough and wrapped in rags. The thing is, the shepherds were the lowliest class of people around. If something was stolen from your home or property in those days, you might look warily and with suspicion on a group of shepherds passing through. Shepherds were the unlikely first visitors of an unlikely newborn King.

The miracle of Incarnation, of God uniting with human flesh, is an act of divine condescension. Normally we think of the word *condescending* as a negative word, as in someone speaking in a condescending way, patronizingly letting you know they are lowering themselves to your level. But, according to the dictionary, the most basic definition includes no negativity. The root word *con* means "together," and *descend* means "to come down." God's condescension simply means that he came down so we could be together with him. It means that he bent to our level; he stooped low from the thing that made him God and took on the things that make us human.

In order to be with us, God limited himself—the Creator stooped to meet the level of creation. But he didn't stop there! God didn't become a human with high status or wealth or power; he became *powerless*: "He made himself nothing / by taking the very nature of a servant" (Philippians

2:7 NIV). Think of it: the Creator and Master of all things became a servant—the person of lowest status in society!

The idea of Jesus's lowliness bringing him to recognize the dignity and worth of even the lowliest human brings us back to the particular miracles, the ones we've been studying together for the last five chapters. If the Grand Miracle of the Incarnation means that every person matters to Jesus—especially those who are in dire and desperate need—then we can see this work itself out in the miracles he performs.

When we look at miracles through this lens, we see that the desperate receive help, the downtrodden are lifted up, and the untouchable feel a touch from Jesus. However, those who approach Jesus in pride and entitlement are not yet at the level to meet the God who has stooped to meet them. Not only the "particular miracles" we've seen Jesus offer one by one to people in need but also the Grand Miracle of the Incarnation—the miracle offered to each and every one of us. God's people, his beloved children, were in a state of despair and desperation, and he moved heaven and earth in order to bend low to be with us. He gave everything, even himself, to buy our ransom and accomplish our rescue.

Sometimes people talk about being in "incarnational ministry." By this they usually mean that they are somehow moving closer to people to whom they want to minister and are entering their world in order to share Christ with them. I want to invite you to think about ways you are being called to display the same kind of love Jesus did what we read about earlier in Philippians 2:7. He put his own needs, status, and preferences on a back burner in order to come close to us. Paul invites us to enter into this way of being: "In your relationships with one another, have the same mindset as Christ Jesus" (Philippians 2:5 NIV).

The Incarnation isn't just about Christmas; it's about every moment when we find ourselves in deep need of a savior. But it does make me think again of that first Christmas morning with the animals around the manger. Whatever season it may be as you are reading this, I hope that preparation will begin in your heart for a perfect Christmas next time December rolls around. Not the kind of perfect achieved with the perfectly decorated house and the perfectly wrapped presents but the perfectly humbled heart prepared to receive a God who would stoop so low that a young woman would scoop him to her breast and hold him tight.

The hope of the Christ child on that first Christmas night held the miracle of Creation restored. God's rescue plan in Jesus set in motion the restoration of the fallen world—wrong made right, sin forgiven, broken things restored, and death undone.

The Miracle of Creation Raised Up

I'm a crier. I cry mostly in happy moments, such as when I see something remarkable in my children's faces or when I'm overwhelmed by the blessings in my life that I've done nothing to deserve. One day my daughter was crying, and I explained that Mommy cries sometimes too. She was curious, since she doesn't usually see me fall down and hurt myself or wake up scared in the night—her usual reasons for crying. As I told her about some of the reasons I cry, she exclaimed, "Oh! You cry for goodness!"

One night it happened as we were reading the story of the Fall in her children's Bible, retold from the account in Genesis 3. As Adam and Eve broke God's rule and ate the fruit they shouldn't have, what might have been an unhappy ending to this particular story ended with a promise of God's forever love and longing for them—and their longing for him and the home he had created:

> You see no matter what, in spite of everything, God would love his children—with a Never Stopping, Never Giving Up, Unbreaking, Always and Forever Love.
>
> And though they would forget him, and run from him, deep in their hearts God's children would miss him always, and long for him—lost children yearning for their home.[7]

As I read that part, my voice just about stopped altogether. I was crying for goodness again.

In the Grand Miracle of God coming to earth in human flesh, the Incarnation, we witness the "Never Stopping, Never Giving Up, Unbreaking, Always and Forever Love" of God in its ultimate form. God is Pursuer, Rescuer, Savior. Some people don't realize that the Incarnation was not the beginning of God's rescue plan in Jesus but the culmination. This plan had been unfolding long before God walked with human feet on creation.

One reason the Incarnation is not the beginning of God's rescue plan is that God had been pursuing his children throughout history. He called to them through every possible means, both pleasing and difficult, for humanity to receive his love. God's self-giving love had been chasing after his people ever since that moment he searched out his shame-filled and hiding children in the garden, calling out "Where are you?" (Genesis 3:8) with the voice of a concerned parent searching for a lost child.

Another reason the Incarnation is not the beginning of God's rescue plan is that it's not Jesus's beginning—only his debut. What do I mean by that? Jesus, as a part of the Trinity—the one-God-in-three-persons Father, Son, and Holy Spirit—is eternal, without beginning or end. Before any human person could see him, there had always been a divine Son of God, even before he became a human being.

The Son was present before the world was created, and the moment he united with human flesh to become 100 percent God and 100 percent human was simply his visible debut on earth, an earth that he created. In coming to us where we are, God continues his miraculous work through forgiveness, adoption, blessing, and restoration. The curse of sin is broken. Those who accept his Son are welcomed into the family of God. We can see ourselves and others through the eyes of God, and even creation itself is part of the restoration plan.

We've seen how God bent low; now let's briefly explore the miracle of how God raises up creation itself in four miracles clustered together.

1. The Miracle of Our Sins Forgiven

God's Grand Miracle in human flesh made a way for our sins to be forgiven in Jesus's sacrifice for us. When Jesus became human, he did something no human had ever done. He did not sin. This helps us understand God's original design for humans—a life without sin—and to see that God wants us to confess our own sins and find forgiveness in him.

Here is the Grand Miracle of our sins forgiven in Jesus: because sin came from a human, only a human could offer a sacrifice that could satisfy the cost of sin—which, according to Romans 6:23, is death. But at the same time, only God was able to undo the curse brought on by Adam and Eve's sin and seen in every human life since. So the only One who was both human and God could make this miracle of sin forgiven a reality for us.

2. The Miracle of Our Adoption as Heirs

The Grand Miracle of the Incarnation means not only that are our sins are forgiven but also that there is an end to our alienation from God and our adoption into his family. You are God's child and heir. I am God's child and heir. Remember how Jairus felt about his cherished only daughter? Remember how Jesus felt about the woman who was healed? This is how God feels about *you*, his child!

God lowers himself so that he can raise us up to become unified with him, to become part of his family.

3. The Miracle of the Blessing of Humankind

The Grand Miracle of the Incarnation means a deep blessing on what it means to be human. Because God chose to unite God and humanity in Jesus Christ, who we are is forever bound up with who God is. It forever changes how we see ourselves and our relationship with God.

Jason Byassee writes, "When God becomes human we can no longer think of God or humanity the same way. God is forever one person.

All persons are now forever tinged with the divine. Everything that is ever good, holy, or beautiful in any human being who has ever lived is already a reflection of the goodness, holiness, and beauty of God."[8]

Whenever we see another person, we can know that God loved them enough to become like them. This changes our capacity to love them as well—and to love the human we see in the mirror!

4. The Miracle of Creation Restored

The Incarnation gives us a new lens of love through which to see ourselves and other human beings, since God united with the flesh of humanity in Jesus Christ. But God doesn't stop there! Jesus is not only human but also a part of creation.

When sin entered the world, Adam and Eve and our human family were not the only ones damaged. The entire creation was reduced from its original state to a now damaged existence.

One of my favorite Advent carols, "Joy to the World," talks about the restoration of all of creation to its original dignity and blessing through the birth of Jesus:

> No more let sins and sorrows grow,
> nor thorns infest the ground;
> he comes to make his blessings flow
> far as the curse is found.[9]

In Jesus, God unites with his creation in a way that says he has not abandoned it but is committed to its full restoration. The Incarnation shows that it is right to delight in creation, because God delights in creation. The Incarnation shows why Christians have been leaders in the arts, sciences, and all fields of knowledge that explore creation. The Incarnation affirms our role and obligation to care for a creation that God did not abandon but united with in flesh.

The Synod of Alexandria, held in AD 360, stated that "Only that which

God becomes is healed."[10] The good news is that God united with creation, so all of his creation will be healed in the coming of his kingdom.

There is no human desperation that Jesus does not understand.

In the miracles of Jesus, God did not offer simply spiritual, invisible blessing. He touched the stuff of earth and made it healed and whole. He multiplied bread, gave sight to blind eyes, walked on water, and touched lepers. These are tangible parts of creation that God calls "good," just as in the first days of Creation. But he blesses his creation by uniting his own Son with the earth that he made and loves.

Doesn't the reality of God's love for his world give you new eyes to see and a new love for a world on which God bestowed a deep blessing by becoming flesh? Praise God: the Creator stooped to become creature in order to restore his creation. He did that for you and for me! And he didn't stop there. God stooped to meet us where we are, die for our sins, and then, in the miracle of all miracles, rise to life again.

The Miracle of Resurrection

The connection between Christmas and Easter, between birth and death and resurrection, is an undeniable one. For Jesus to be truly human, he had to die. For Jesus to defeat death, he had to be divine. Jesus as 100 percent human and 100 percent God is fully realized in his death and resurrection.

One of my favorite stories that parallels the miracle of resurrection is C. S. Lewis's fantasy series *The Chronicles of Narnia*. On one level, this series is about an imaginary world called Narnia, where animals talk, battles are fought, and magical spells are made and broken. The lion called Aslan is a strong and valiant king of the realm, a huge lion who captures his imagination. But the story is so much more, because C. S. Lewis wrote Aslan as an illustration of Jesus: strong and valiant but also forgiving and humble, willing to sacrifice his own life for children even when they act their worst.

In *The Lion, the Witch, and the Wardrobe*, Aslan actually lays down his life for the most treacherous of the children. When the child has betrayed his own family and friends, the witch of the story reminds them that she is owed the traitor's blood. Aslan makes a deal with her that she can have his blood in exchange and then goes willingly with her as he is tied down, his magnificent mane is shaved, and then he is killed. I read this part to my son Drew, and I'm not sure how I made it through that part of the story, because I cried all the way! The truth of Jesus laying down his life for us was just too overwhelming, moving me in a whole new way as I read aloud to my son, who I hope will someday understand what it means that Jesus died for him.

As we've seen, the greatest miracle of all is who Jesus is; every other miracle flows from that reality. Other "particular miracles" are signs that point us to Jesus himself, our only permanent gift. But, ultimately, Jesus's death and resurrection were really the fulfillment of his incarnation.

What do I mean by that? Well, for Jesus to be fully human, he had to experience the full range of human experience, which for every human being that has ever lived has meant death. As someone once put it: no matter how science advances, the death rate is 100 percent—it never goes up or down! So, for Jesus to be fully human, he had to die.

Even in his death, Jesus identified with the greatest suffering and injustice of the world. Instead of a quick or painless death, Jesus's death would mean no one could claim he was immune to any kind of human sorrow.

The prophet Isaiah named the purpose of Jesus's suffering for us well, relating his suffering to our healing:

> Surely he has borne our infirmities
> and carried our diseases;
> yet we accounted him stricken,

> struck down by God, and afflicted.
> But he was wounded for our transgressions,
>   crushed for our iniquities;
> upon him was the punishment that made us whole,
>   and by his bruises we are healed. (Isaiah 53:4-5)

At the moment of Jesus's death, the curtain in the temple was ripped in two from top to bottom. This curtain divided the holy place from the most holy place or Holy of Holies, where God's presence was thought to live; and its tearing from top to bottom communicated that because Jesus had taken our sins and our punishment on himself in his death, no division would ever need to exist again between God and his people.

Three days later, when Jesus rose from the dead, another opening was created—the opening of the door to death that had locked humanity behind it since the day humans were exiled from the garden of Eden. C. S. Lewis put it this way: "He has forced open a door that has been locked since the death of the first man. He has met, fought, and beaten the King of Death. Everything is different because He has done so. This is the beginning of the New Creation: a new chapter in cosmic history has opened."[11]

The ultimate understanding of Jesus's identity came at the moments of his crucifixion and his resurrection:

"Truly this man was God's Son!" (Matthew 27:54)

He was shown to be the Son of God when he was raised from the dead by the power of the Holy Spirit. He is Jesus Christ our Lord. (Romans 1:4 NLT)

So Jesus's death meant that he experienced the worst of human experience; he had walked our earth, experienced our pain, and died our death. But his resurrection from the dead meant that the human experience would not have to end at death. The miracle of Jesus's resurrection meant that we would be offered resurrection as well.

Reading C. S. Lewis's books about Narnia to my son somehow made me weep over Jesus's death and resurrection in ways I hadn't done in years. The great lion Aslan had given his life for a traitor when he didn't deserve death. Two young girls had witnessed that death and then were the first to meet the resurrected Aslan—just like the women at the garden tomb who met Jesus. Here are the lines I read to my son through tears:

> "Oh, you're real, you're real! Oh, Aslan!" cried Lucy and both girls flung themselves upon him and covered him with kisses.
> "But what does it all mean?" asked Susan when they were somewhat calmer.
> "It means," said Aslan, "that though the Witch knew the Deep Magic, there is a magic deeper still which she did not know. Her knowledge goes back only to the dawn of Time. But if she could have looked a little further back, into the stillness and the darkness before Time dawned, she would have read there a different incantation. She would have known that when a willing victim who has committed no treachery was killed in a traitor's stead, the Table would crack and Death itself would start working backwards. And now—"
> "Oh yes. Now?" said Lucy jumping up and clapping her hands....
> "And now," said Aslan presently, "to business. I feel I am going to roar."[12]

The beauty of the Grand Miracle of Jesus is only a complete picture when we see his life, death, and resurrection as the way that he showed up for a desperate world and gave everything—even his own life.

Hope for Tomorrow

Our moments of desperation when God was enough for us—when nothing else was—can bring the spirit of yesterday's desperation forward into today and keep us in touch with the fact that although we desperately need God, we do not have to live desperate lives in order to receive this miracle of Jesus. He doesn't want our lives to be chaotic and crazy; he simply wants our hearts to be surrendered to him. Having a desperate heart means that we remember we need Jesus on our best day as much as we did on our worst day. And it means that we always have hope for tomorrow.

The very same power that God exerted when he raised Christ from the dead is the same power we've been dipping our toes into as we've walked together through the miracles of Jesus—the power that healed lepers, calmed storms, fed thousands, and met and answered the desperation of even the smallest and most undeserving persons. What could it mean that this power is at work in those who believe? What a grand miracle, indeed, that the same power that raised Christ and defeated death is here surrounding you right now!

The Grand Miracle is that God would choose to come and live among us and occupy not only our best moments but also our most difficult ones. Jesus so fully entered the human experience, the fullness of God participating in the fullness of humanity, that he experienced not only the joy but also the most painful, uncomfortable, humiliating parts of what it means to be human. From the very start, as a baby, he was needy and dependent on others. And to his very end on the cross, he was despised and rejected, executed in the most humiliating way.

God entered our most desperate human conditions. He became desperate in order to rescue us from our desperation. Jesus was born as a dependent baby, he died on a desperate cross, and God amazingly rescued humanity when Jesus defeated death through the resurrection—Jesus is the Grand Miracle. And all the other miracles we've witnessed point to him.

You and I are part of this ongoing, unfolding miracle. When we gather together in groups to study and pray together, we're part of the Grand Miracle of Jesus. When we worship in gatherings of those who believe in him, we're part of the reunion of the rescued—a part of the unfolding miracle of his death and resurrection.

Life as a rescued people doesn't mean that we live in a perfect world now. You and I are going to have good days and bad days, but we remember, too, that we're the people of the cross. And because of the cross of Jesus, because of the desperation that overcame death, our worst day actually becomes our best. It is a rescue story so old, but it becomes new every time someone is rescued. As those who have been rescued, we long to see the miracle generate new miracles. We love the joy of seeing the next person brought to life and restored to wholeness and joy. You and I are little miracles—lives saved and restored, all because of the Grand Miracle of who Jesus is.

Jesus walked in our shoes on this earth, and he entered our human desperation in order to rescue us. This Grand Miracle not only gives us hope for every circumstance but also enables us to be participants in God's rescue of others. We have the privilege of sharing with others the hope of the greatest miracle of all, our rescuer Jesus. He is the Miracle we're all searching for.

FORTY-DAY READING PLAN

I f you would like to use this book as a daily devotional and delve deeper into the Scriptures, here is a forty-day plan to read the chapters in this book, explore the referenced Scriptures more deeply, and reflect on some personal applications these stories and Scriptures might have for your own life with Jesus. Find a journal or notebook to make notes, copy Scripture verses that are speaking to you, and write out your reflections to the questions each day.

Day 1: Read chapter 1.

Day 2: Read Mark 7:25-26; 9:17-18, 24; Luke 18:35-38; John 5:1-9; 11:21. Where do you see desperation? In the miracle stories, people come to the end of themselves—running out of ideas, options, strength, and resources—and Jesus steps in to make things right.

Day 3: Read John 2:1-12. How are the water, wine, and wedding signs that Jesus uses to point us to something deeper? Signs exist to call our attention to something more important, to act as the guide to what we are looking for. John tells miracle stories to point us to Jesus.

Day 4: Read John 2:5. How would the story be different if the servants had decided to take matters into their own hands? Listening for instruction and then doing God's will means we're putting the whole messy situation in God's hands, acknowledging that we are simply the servants of his will.

Day 5: Read John 2:1-12 as though you have never heard the story. What jumps out at you? What questions do you have for Jesus? What might God be speaking to you about through this miracle story?

Day 6: Look up some instances of how obedience leads to a miracle: Exodus 14:21; 17:5-6, 9-10. How does God use something Moses already has in each of these miraculous events?

Day 7: Read Job 38:25-28, 37-38; Psalm 113:5-6; Matthew 16:15; Mark 4:41. When have you said to yourself, "Who is like our God?"

Day 8: Read chapter 2.

Day 9: Read 1 Samuel 17:48-50; 1 Kings 18:41-46; 19:11-13; Matthew 13:31-32; James 3:5. How are small things used in big ways? The scarcity of the ingredients reminds us that it's God's power, not human ingenuity or provision, to which we should give our attention and praise.

Day 10: Read Mark 6:30-44. When have you laid out your scarcity or shortage before God, showing him just how impossible things look? When blessed in Jesus's hands, the five loaves and two fish turn out to be a feast. Jesus actually divides five loaves among all of them, and then amazingly he divides the two fish among them all.

Day 11: Read John 6:32-35. What is Jesus saying about bread? God provides for all of our needs. It doesn't always make sense. We can't always figure out how he will do it. We don't always understand his methods. But he will always be there to meet our needs. God always provides.

Day 12: Read Matthew 4:1-4. Where do you see any scarcity and desperation in Jesus's temptation? How does Jesus respond?

Day 13: Read 1 Kings 17:13-16. Can you think of a time God provided for your needs just when you thought you had run out? The miracle story in the New Testament of the feeding of the five thousand also echoes one of the greatest stories of abundance found in Scripture: the encounter of the prophet Elijah and the widow of Zarephath.

Day 14: Read Luke 5:1-11. When have you ever said to God, "OK, if you say so. . ."? We try everything we can in our own strength, and we only find failure, so Jesus is a last resort. The good news is that Jesus doesn't reject us just because we take a while to do it his way!

Day 15: Read chapter 3.

Day 16: Read Mark 4:35-41. What do we learn about the storm? What does Jesus say to the sea? When we are in the midst of extremely hard times, it's so easy to question whether God cares. These disciples had witnessed Jesus going out of his way to heal and help and save so many people from danger and distress.

Day 17: Read Genesis 1:2 and Revelation 15:2. What does the water symbolize? Each of Jesus's miracles in some way combats the evil powers of the world and shows that God is triumphant over them.

Day 18: Read Matthew 14:28. Where do you sense a desire for God to call you out of the ordinary? We all have them in our lives: places where we live day in and day out, going through the everyday, boring motions. We forget sometimes that the ordinary places are also where the extra-ordinary is most likely to happen.

Day 19: Read John 21:1-11. What would you have done if you were in the boat that night? The first time, the miraculous presence of a holy God causes Peter to notice his own sin. But later, after all they've been through together, Peter actually drops everything, including the catch!

Day 20: Read Mark 6:45-52 a few times. What sticks out to you as you read the miracle story? What might God be saying to you through this passage?

Day 21: Read chapter 4.

Day 22: Read Luke 5:12-16. What things do you need to take boldly to Jesus, expecting that he can give you the healing you seek? God wants *you* to approach him with bold humility and offer him your needs. He wants you to know that there's nothing so damaged in your life (or the lives of others) that it would deter him from touching you.

Day 23: Read Mark 2:1-11. What is special about the act of friendship in this story? Who are your friends that carry you to Jesus? In community, sometimes we are those who carry, and sometimes we are those who are carried.

Day 24: Read Psalm 133:1; Luke 10:30-37; Galatians 6:1-10. How does a community who bears each other's burdens point to God? The Bible paints a picture of community where our burdens are not our own. They are to be shared with others when needed but never in a way that is unhealthy or exempts us from personal responsibility.

Day 25: Read Mark 9:14-29. The father expresses a desire to believe wholeheartedly in Jesus, while at the same time he confesses a cautious, tentative hope. He has faith, but yet he lacks faith. If we're honest, most of us in our greatest moments of need could say the same thing to God. We are a people who have faith and need faith all at once. When has this been true for you?

Day 26: Read Luke 12:7. What does this verse tell you about God's love and care for you? God knows the number of hairs on our heads, and although he pays attention to the tiniest of birds, we are worth more than a whole flock of them! When you wonder if God sees you, hears you, and cares about you and your concerns, remember that it's just not possible for God to forget about you.

Day 27: Read Mark 7:24-30. What do you learn about desperation? According to the Gospel of Mark, Jesus wins every controversial conversation he has with the religious authorities, yet he allows himself to be persuaded by this desperate parent. Take that in for a moment. Desperate persistence moves the heart of God!

Day 28: Read Mark 7:29-30. What is the result of the woman's persistence? Have you ever come to God with such desperation and persistence?

Day 29: Read chapter 5.

Day 30: Read Mark 5:21-37. What jumps out at you in this passage? What are the similarities between the two miracles in this passage?

Day 31: Read 1 Corinthians 15:54-55 and Revelation 21:4. What do they say about death? What does it say about God that he would send Jesus to defeat death? God began the world as a place where death had no place in the unspoiled creation that was his perfect will. In order to return his people to a place with no more death or mourning or crying or pain, Jesus undertook a comprehensive campaign of war against death itself!

Day 32: Read Mark 5:41-42; Luke 7:14-15; and John 11:43-44. Even though Jesus raises these people from the dead, eventually they die. How does that broaden your idea of what a miracle looks like?

Day 33: Read Mark 1:41-42; 9:14-27; Luke 5:12-16; 7:11-15. When have you known Jesus's compassion in your life? In the Gospels, Jesus feels and acts on compassion by moving toward the people he encounters who are in deep need. Before many of the miracles, Jesus displays or is described as having this compassion that leads to action.

Day 34: Read Psalm 41:3 and 2 Corinthians 12:7-10. How is God's grace sufficient for our struggles? We know not everyone will be healed in our "not yet" world. We know that not everything will look or function the way God wants it to. We know that we will find ourselves desperate for Jesus to work a miracle.

Day 35: Read chapter 6.

Day 36: Read Luke 1:26-38. What are some of the promises of God's presence and power? In Jesus, God and humanity have become one. How can this even be possible? To define God is to paint categories that are outside of human possibility. He is without limits in his knowledge (omniscience), location (omnipresence), and power (omnipotence).

Day 37: Read Luke 2:4-12. How did God enter the world? God's condescension means that he came down so we could be together. It means that he bent to our level, that he stooped low from the thing that made him God and took on the things that make us human.

Day 38: Read Matthew 8:1-3; 15:21-28. How did Jesus bend low to meet a need?

Day 39: Read 2 Corinthians 8:9. What is the exchange of riches between Jesus and humankind?

Day 40: Read Galatians 4:4-7. What is the deep blessing on what it means to be human? The Grand Miracle of the Incarnation means a deep blessing on what it means to be human. Because God chose to unite God and humanity in Jesus Christ, who we are is forever bound up with who God is. It forever changes how we see ourselves and our relationship with God.

NOTES

1. The Gift of Desperation

1. "Miracles" in *Dictionary of Jesus and the Gospels,* ed. Joel Green, Scot McKnight, and I. Howard Marshall (Downers Grove, IL: InterVarsity, 1992), 872.

2. Timothy Keller, *Encounters with Jesus: Unexpected Answers to Life's Biggest Questions* (New York: Penguin, 2013), 59.

3. Kamila Blessing, *Families of the Bible: A New Perspective* (Santa Barbara, CA: Praeger, 2010), 41.

4. Craig S. Keener, *The IVP Bible Background Commentary: New Testament,* 2nd ed. (Downer's Grove, IL: InterVarsity, 2014), 253.

2. The Miracle of Abundance

1. Stuart Briscoe, *Brave Enough to Follow: What Jesus Can Do When You Keep Your Eyes on Him* (Colorado Springs: NavPress, 2004), 76.

2. Mark Buchanan, *Your God Is Too Safe: Rediscovering the Wonder of a God You Can't Control* (Colorado Springs: Multnomah, 2001), 39.

3. James Martin, *Jesus: A Pilgrimage* (San Francisco: HarperOne, 2016), 258.

4. "Bethsaida," *New American Standard Exhaustive Concordance of the Bible* (La Habra, CA: Lockman, 1998), http://biblehub.com/greek/966.htm.

5. "Gospels" in *Dictionary of Jesus and the Gospels*, ed. Joel Green, Scot McKnight, and I. Howard Marshall (Downers Grove, IL: InterVarsity, 1992), 294.

6. Buchanan, *Your God Is Too Safe*, 38.

7. Arland J. Hultgren, "Commentary on Luke 5:1-11," *Working Preacher*, February 7, 2010, www.workingpreacher.org/preaching.aspx? commentary_id=506.

3. Miracles on the Water

1. Todd Bolen, "Jesus and the Sea of Galilee," first published in *Bible and Spade* magazine (Fall 2003); reprinted on their website Associates for Biblical Research, March 6, 2009, www.biblearchaeology.org/post/2009/03/Jesus -and-the-Sea-of-Galilee.aspx.

2. James Boyce, "Commentary on Mark 4:35-41," *Working Preacher*, June 21, 2015, www.workingpreacher.org/preaching.aspx?commentary_id=2470.

3. David E. Garland, *The NIV Application Commentary: Mark* (Grand Rapids, MI: Zondervan, 1996), 263.

4. Scott Walker, *Footsteps of the Fisherman: With St. Peter on the Path of Discipleship* (Minneapolis: Augsburg Fortress, 2003), 35.

5. Dr. Frank Stagg, quoted in Walker, *Footsteps of the Fisherman*, 37.

4. Jesus Our Healer

1. Mark Pearson, *Christian Healing: A Practical and Comprehensive Guide* (Lake Mary, FL: Charisma House, 2004), 4.

2. *New American Standard Exhaustive Concordance of the Bible*, s.v. "baros" (La Habra, CA: Lockman, 1998), http://biblehub.com/greek/922.htm.

3. *New American Concordance of the Bible*, s.v. "phortion," http://biblehub .com/greek/5413.htm.

4. Craig S. Keener, "Mark 7:24-30," *The IVP Bible Background Commentary: New Testament*, 2nd ed. (Downer's Grove, IL: InterVarsity, 2014), 146.

5. A Two-for-One Miracle Story

1. *The Princess Bride*, directed by Rob Reiner, written by William Goldman (Beverly Hills, CA: Act III Communications, 1987).

2. Many of these points of similarity are found in Joseph R. Dongell, *The Gospel of Mark, Onebook: The Biblical Journey* (Franklin, TN: Seedbed, 2015), 91.

3. Dongell, *Gospel of Mark*, 91.

4. Dongell, *Gospel of Mark*, 91.

5. Stephen Seamands in Theology and Practice of Healing class (TH 635) at Asbury Theological Seminary (Fall 2015).

6. Spiros Zodhiates, ed., *The Complete Word Study Dictionary: New Testament* (Chattanooga: Zondervan, 1992), 1305.

6. The Grand Miracle

1. Ben Witherington, "The Meaning of Incarnation," Patheos, December 23, 2012, www.patheos.com/blogs/bibleandculture/2012/12/23/the-meaning-of-incarnation/.

2. W. E. Vine, "John 1:14," *W. E. Vine's New Testament Word Pictures, Matthew to Acts*, ed. Martin H. Manser (Nashville: Thomas Nelson, 2015), 615.

3. "The Apostles' Creed, Traditional Version," *The United Methodist Hymnal* (Nashville: The United Methodist Publishing House, 1989), 881.

4. "The Apostles' Creed, Ecumenical Version," *United Methodist Hymnal*, 882.

5. C. S. Lewis, *Miracles* (first published 1947; New York: HarperCollins, 2001), 173–74.

6. Max Lucado, *God Came Near* (Nashville: Thomas Nelson, 2004), 4.

7. Sally Lloyd-Jones, "The Terrible Lie" in *The Story of God's Love for You* (Grand Rapids, MI: Zondervan, 2015).

8. Jason Byassee, *Trinity: The God We Don't Know* (Nashville: Abingdon Press, 2015), 74.

9. Isaac Watts, "Joy to the World," *United Methodist Hymnal*, 246.

10. "The Synod of Alexandria," quoted by Robert E. Webber in *Ancient-Future Faith: Rethinking Evangelicalism for a Postmodern World* (Grand Rapids, MI: Baker, 1999), 65.

11. Lewis, *Miracles*, 236–37.

12. C. S. Lewis, *The Lion, the Witch, and the Wardrobe* (New York: Collier, 1970), 159–60.

ABOUT THE AUTHOR

Jessica LaGrone is dean of the Chapel at Asbury Theological Seminary in Wilmore, Kentucky, and an acclaimed pastor, teacher, and speaker whose engaging communication style endears her to groups and audiences throughout the United States. A native of Texas, Jessica previously served as pastor of Creative Ministries at The Woodlands United Methodist Church near Houston, Texas. She is the author of numerous studies including *Set Apart: Holy Habits of Prophets and Kings; Broken and Blessed: How God Used One Imperfect Family to Change the World;* and *Namesake: When God Rewrites Your Story.* She also is the author of one book, also titled *Broken and Blessed: God Changes the World One Person and One Family at a Time,* a contributor to the all-church Advent study *Under Wraps: The Gift We Never Expected,* and a video host for DISCIPLE *Fast Track: Becoming Disciples Through Bible Study.* Jessica and her husband, Jim, have two young children, Drew and Kate.

Follow Jessica:

 @JessicaLaGrone

 @jixsalagrone

 @jessicalagrone

Her Blog JessicaLaGrone.com

More from Jessica LaGrone

Bible Studies

The Miracles of Jesus: Finding God in Desperate Moments
Workbook ISBN: 9781501835452

Participate in a captivating examination of the miracles of Jesus in this six-week Bible study. Join LaGrone as she leads us in exploring miracle stories such as turning water into wine, feeding the 5,000, various miracles on the water, five stories of healing, death and resurrection, and the Incarnation as we work towards inviting God to work powerfully in our life.

Set Apart: Holy Habits of Prophets and Kings
Workbook ISBN: 9781426778421

Examine the holy habits of six kings and prophets who were set apart by their close walk with God. Each week you'll study the story of one intriguing character, discuss God's unique purpose for his life, and learn about his particular spiritual discipline. Then you'll explore how that timeless spiritual practice can draw you closer to God, helping you fulfill God's purpose for your life.

Broken and Blessed: How God Used One Imperfect Family to Change the World
Workbook ISBN: 9781426778377

See how God brings blessings from our brokenness.

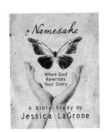

Namesake: When God Rewrites Your Story
Workbook ISBN: 9781426761874

Discover people in Scripture whose lives and names were changed forever by God.

Book

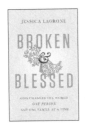

Broken & Blessed: God Changes the World One Person and One Family at a Time
Trade Book ISBN: 9781426774911

Meet the first family in Genesis who was a mess by anyone's standards. God chose them for his purpose just as he chooses us and our families today.

DVD, leader guide, and kit also available for each six-week study.
Discover samples of her book and Bible studies at AbingdonWomen.com/JessicaLaGrone

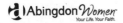